THE CHAMBER PLAYS

OF
AUGUST STRINDBERG

TRANSLATED BY
PAUL WALSH

The Chamber Plays of August Strindberg

Translated by Paul Walsh
Copyright © 2012 by Paul Walsh
All rights reserved

Published by EXIT PRESS
Assistance for EXIT Press was provided by the
Kenneth R. Rainin Foundation

The translation of *The Black Glove* was supported by the
Swedish Arts Council

Book design by Richard Livingston

CAUTION: Professionals and amateurs are hereby warned that all plays represented in this book are subject to a royalty. They are fully protected under the copyright laws of the United States of America, and of all countries covered by the International Copyright Union (including the Dominion of Canada and the rest of the British Commonwealth), and of all countries with which the United States has reciprocal copyright relations. All rights, including professional, amateur, motion picture, recitation, lecturing, public reading, radio broadcasting, television, and the rights of translation into foreign languages, are strictly reserved.

All inquiries concerning rights for readings, productions, etc, should be addressed to:
Abrams Artists Agency
275 Seventh Avenue, 26th Floor
New York, NY 10001
Attn: Morgan Jenness
Morgan.Jenness@abramsartny.com

For additional information about
EXIT PRESS, go to
www.exitpress.org

Paperback ISBN: 978-0-9774684-8-5
E-book ISBN: 978-0-9774684-9-2

EXIT PRESS
156 Eddy Street
San Francisco, CA 94102-2708
mail@theexit.org
distributed by Small Press Distribution spdbooks.org

First Edition: October 2012

Contents

Foreword
by Paul Walsh v

Introduction
by Rob Melrose ix

Storm 1

Burned House 45

The Ghost Sonata 91

The Pelican 133

The Black Glove 175

Notes 211

About the Translator 219

Foreword

Since the middle of the last century, Strindberg has been heralded as the father of modern drama. For many, however, he has been a kind of absentee father: little seen, little known, and little appreciated. We have read a handful of his plays, and occasionally have had the opportunity to see a few of them produced. But for the most part Strindberg remains an enigma: scary, dour, and formidable. Today a new generation is encountering Strindberg for the first time and they find him fascinating, like an eccentric grandfather: surprising in his depth and breadth of experience, shocking in the intimacy of his revelations, startling in the reach of his imagination. They find him daring and outlandish, but also familiar and sometimes magical. It's this strange quality of being constantly remade by the world he tried so desperately to understand that makes Strindberg seem always of our time and perhaps a step ahead. And it's this that keeps us coming back.

The Chamber Plays

Strindberg began writing his chamber plays early in 1907 for a group of young actors under the leadership of August Falck who were embarking on a new endeavor: to open a small theater in the center of Stockholm dedicated to the plays of August Strindberg. The theater would be called *Intima Teatern* (The Intimate Theater), and it would explore the possibilities of a new kind of drama for the new century. Between January and June 1907, Strindberg composed the first four of his chamber plays. Early in 1909 he added *The Black Glove*, which he called Opus 5 of the chamber plays.

In his *Open Letters to the Intimate Theater*, Strindberg provides a memorable definition of a chamber play: "The name itself suggests its hidden program," Strindberg wrote: "The idea of chamber music brought into the drama: an intimate experience, a meaningful motif, a meticulous treatment. . . . No predetermined form should bind the author, for the motif should command the form. In other words: freedom of treatment, bound only by the unity of the conception and the tone." Here was a recipe for experiment. It embraced the possibilities of intimate revelations, unbound by conventional notions of dramatic form and structure, to provide the audience with an intimate experience and an experience of intimacy.

These days, we tend to think of an intimate play as a small play: two or three characters revealing something about themselves and about life. Strindberg preferred a larger canvas. In fact, none of Strindberg's chamber plays fits very comfortably in a chamber, with the possible exception of *The Pelican*. These are not small plays. There are too many characters, too many locations, too many scenographic demands. *Burned House* and *The Ghost Sonata*, for example, each have fourteen roles; *The Ghost Sonata* has three detailed locales including the opening street scene before the two-story façade of a building with people appearing on the upper balcony and coming out the front door. Each of the five scenes of *The Black Glove* takes place in a different location within a modern six-story apartment building; sometimes multiple locations are visible simultaneously. No, these are not small plays, nor do they fit comfortably in a chamber.

As Strindberg defined the genre, a chamber play offers an experience of intimacy not smallness, and intimacy is about a quality of self-revelation. The Stranger's encounter with himself in *Burned House*, for example, by way of each of the people he meets from his past, allows for a particular journey of self-examination that would not be possible with fewer characters. The journey of the student in *The Ghost Sonata* into the Hyacinth Room — and his discovery that what he had thought was paradise is in fact another prison house — would not be possible without the complex scenic demands that Strindberg places upon the play. Even a deceptively simple play like *Storm* demands a complex set in which characters and audience can watch a private life suddenly revealed through the ground-floor windows of the Gentleman's apartment. What makes these plays extraordinary is that Strindberg is a generous collaborator, leaving room for actors and directors to discover new ways into these plays and new ways to produce them.

Translating these plays for Cutting Ball Theater's ambitious Strindberg Centennial project (production of all five of Strindberg's chamber plays in repertory), I've been struck by the similarity of concerns in the plays as a group, and also by shared strategies of development and effect. As a group, these plays offer a complex and compelling meditation on notions of intimacy, both in life and in the theater. Each deals with intimate feelings associated with loss and death and jealousy. And each has a tone of melancholy and loss that sometimes turns bitter but always seeks to reconcile the audience to the unfathomable mysteries of life. In the process, these enigmatic little plays structure an experience that invites audiences to postpone the search for meaning and embrace instead a dialogue of self-revelation. They violate assumptions about dramatic action while challenging assumptions about privacy in modern life. And each relies on the close proximity of the audience to the action and to the actors. They demand an honesty and directness from the actors that is itself intimate;

an honesty capable of revealing hidden thoughts and private secrets through carefully articulated gestures and subtly modulated rhythms.

Each of these plays shares a sense of interwoven fates and of the stripping away of pretenses and illusions, of imprisonment in the madhouse world with death as liberator, of sleepers awaking and secrets brought to light, and of great conflagrations and collapses. And despite these plays' emphasis on moments of self-revelation and intimate communication, each challenges the efficacy of language itself as a tool of communication. Again and again, language is revealed as an instrument of dissimulation, a weapon of accusation and recrimination, a mask to hide secrets and avoid contact. In this, Strindberg anticipated and precipitated new directions for drama in the 20th century, examining language itself and its power on stage to both create and conceal character.

One of those places where language fails most evidently is in trying to come to terms with the self-deception of jealousy, which plays a central role in each of these plays. Jealousy is such a private and isolating emotion, mixing anxiety with shame and self-doubt with rage, that it can only be observed from a distance as it consumes another. In this, it is like death. Both inscribe their subject in a circle of isolation that is at the heart of the experience that Strindberg wishes to share with his audience. In a letter to his German translator Emil Schering written in April 1907 after Schering had read the first three of the chamber plays and apparently asked for some clarification of the tangled web of relationships and interrelationships depicted in them, Strindberg begged for a bit of discretion *"s'il vous plaît."* After all, he says, "in the chamber plays one doesn't ask your kind of questions!" In this world of lies and illusions "one lives in the world of intimations, where you speak in muted half-tones, because you are ashamed of being a human being!"

That these five plays investigate a cluster of shared themes, motifs and allusions is not surprising, given that they were written in such a concentrated span of time. But each play also creates its own structure and approach. Each is as experimental as the others, from the seemingly conventional realism of Storm to the outlandish dream quality of *The Ghost Sonata* to the lyrical sweetness of *The Black Glove*. And none proposes a clear solution to the problems it reveals. Instead Strindberg embraces the possibility of multiple responses. And this makes his plays perennially modern. A play like *Burned House* is a cynical play to be sure, "hinting at the nothingness of everything, and the glorification of nothingness!" as Strindberg wrote in a letter to Schering. But like the other chamber plays it is redeemed by the candor with which it attempts to probe the hidden recesses of what most often is left unsaid.

There is a lyrical exploration of existential need played out on the periphery of these plays that strikes us today as a revelation. As Strindberg reminds us in these five extraordinary plays, the drama of modern life (what Strindberg in a letter to his publisher called "the style of Art Nouveau") found its voice in the early 20th century by examining those revelations that exist in the margins of the dramatic rather than in a drama of plots and action. Theatrical moments of Aristotelian reversal and recognition may not be the soul of a drama of the soul. That soul may reside in "an intimate experience, a meaningful motif, a meticulous treatment."

Paul Walsh
New Haven
August 2012

Introduction
by Rob Melrose

Strindberg

August Strindberg was an extraordinary human being. If Leonardo da Vinci was the first Renaissance Man then August Strindberg was in many ways our last. He, along with Henrik Ibsen and Anton Chekhov, is one of the three major pioneers of modern realism in the theater with his plays *Miss Julie* and *The Father*. That in and of itself is an achievement worthy of his place in the canon. In addition, he singlehandedly ushered in a new kind of drama that found its inspiration in dreams: *A Dream Play*, *Ghost Sonata*, *To Damascus I, II, III*, *The Keys of Heaven*, and *The Great Highway*. These plays became the prototype for expressionist drama and later of absurdist theater. It is hard to imagine the plays of Tennessee Williams, Edward Albee, Eugene O'Neill, Georg Kaiser, Eugène Ionesco, and Samuel Beckett without August Strindberg.

Strindberg's talents, however, extended far beyond the plays for which he is best known. He was an accomplished novelist. His novel *The Red Room* has been described as the first modern Swedish novel and his autobiographical novels *Inferno* and *Son of a Servant* are considered precursors of the work of Marcel Proust and Franz Kafka. He wrote short stories, essays, and poetry as well. He was also a painter whose bold experiments make his paintings look more like abstract impressionism than they do the other paintings of his day. In auction houses today, his paintings sell for millions of dollars. Strindberg was a photographer who was experimenting even as the art of photography was being born. Sometimes he used a broken lens because he liked the effect it had on his photographs. He was a chemist and an alchemist whose scientific writings gained him access to the laboratories at the Sorbonne while he was in Paris. He was also a botanist and a linguist. Above all, he was a voracious reader and wrote feverishly in the margins of his books which remain in his extensive library at his "Blue Tower" apartment to this day.

This is a monumental artist who is deserving of our attention and study. I am thrilled that one hundred years after his death, we have an excuse for celebrating a Strindberg Centennial and hope that it makes theaters, galleries and publishers realize that we need no excuse to delve into the work of Strindberg regardless of the year. He still has so much to teach us and his influence is everywhere.

Strindberg Cycle: The Chamber Plays in Rep at The Cutting Ball Theater

This book is the result of a dream translator Paul Walsh, Cutting Ball co-founder Paige Rogers and I have had for over a decade: a production of all five of Strindberg's Chamber Plays in Rep. Paul, Paige and I have been Strindberg fans for many years. Paul's doctoral dissertation was on Strindberg's early plays. Paige's undergraduate thesis was on *Miss Julie* and my graduate thesis was on his last play *The Great Highway*. Before I met Paul at the American Conservatory Theater where he was head of dramaturgy and where I was an assistant director, I had read his excellent essay on *The Pelican* in a collection of writings called *Strindberg's Dramaturgy* edited by Strindberg scholar Göran Stockenström and had seen a production of his translation of Strindberg's *Creditors* at Classic Stage Company. A love of Strindberg and a love of theater has been a strong bond for the three of us.

I've always been drawn to Strindberg's Chamber Plays. These are five short plays that Strindberg wrote at the end of his career. At the end of Strindberg's life, he moved back to Stockholm after many years in continental Europe. He founded The Intimate Theater with artistic director August Falck. The Intimate Theater had about 150 seats and had a stage that was 20 feet by 20 feet (about the same size as Cutting Ball's stage) and was to be devoted to the works of Strindberg. The Intimate Theater was created in opposition to the large houses that were common at the time which required a kind of declamatory acting style which Strindberg found unfit for his plays and the kind of intimate acting style that he sought. He called the five plays he wrote specifically for this theater chamber plays as a way of relating them to chamber music. If his other plays were symphonies, then these were to be chamber pieces. He even took up the musical convention of giving a number to each opus: *Storm* – Opus 1, *Burned House* – Opus 2, *The Ghost Sonata* – Opus 3, *The Pelican* – Opus 4, The Black Glove – Opus 5. Some scholars do not consider *The Black Glove* to be one of the Chamber Plays because it was written two years after the others and because it was never performed at the Intimate Theater. For us, the fact that Strindberg calls it Opus 5 means that he considered it one of the Chamber Plays and unequivocally belongs with the others.[1]

These plays experiment with style in bold and exciting ways. They make us question the convention of dividing Strindberg's plays into naturalistic plays and expressionist plays. The Chamber Plays float somewhere in between these two kinds of theater and each in its own particular way. That is what makes them so ideal for Cutting Ball. Our mission since our founding in 1999 has been to create productions of experimental new plays, re-envisioned classics and seminal avant garde works. This means that every play we produce is experimenting with form in some way; each play is redefining what theater should be. We like to surprise and challenge our audience by presenting them with a new form of theater every time they walk through our doors. As we have been working on these plays, our challenge has been to ask ourselves how each of the five plays defines its own notion of theater. To reflect these differences, we want to allow the conventions and the styles to change for each play in the cycle. Strindberg, along with Alfred Jarry (*Ubu Roi*), Georg Büchner (*Woyzeck*), and Maurice Maeterlinck (*Pelleas and Melisande*), is one of the fathers of avant garde theater. For an experimental theater company he is the perfect writer to feature in a large-scale project.

Translator Paul Walsh

Paul Walsh, is the perfect translator for this project. In addition to being an experienced Strindberg scholar and translator, he is a dramaturg and man of the theater who has worked with companies like the Théâtre de la Jeune Lune, The American Conservatory Theater and the New Harmony Project where he was Artistic Director, and has worked with writers such as Mac Wellman and Tom Stoppard. He has a wonderful sense of the possibilities of theater and is in touch with the work that theater artists are creating today. On one hand, he is deeply faithful to Strindberg's words and is tireless in getting it right, on the other hand he has no preconceived notions about how the plays should be done and is endlessly encouraging our company to push our imagination further — beyond conventions and expectations. He felt that we were the right company for this project partly because of our work on plays by Richard Foreman, Mac Wellman and Suzan Lori Parks — something I am only starting to understand now at the early stages of our design and rehearsal process.

These translations are meant for the theater. They are meant to be acted. Paul has spent decades in rehearsals and has a deep sense of the actor's process. He loves being in rehearsal and listens well. When the actors are rehearsing at the table, Paul often has one eye on the Swedish text and another eye on what the actor is doing. He wants to help the actor when a line doesn't quite roll off the tongue and at the same time, he challenges the actor to take on a linguistic challenge that Strindberg has placed in the text on purpose. A favorite example of mine is Paul's translation of the confectioner's line in Storm when he calls the weather "*rötmånadsvärme*" which literally means "the rotting month's warm" and is strange even in Swedish. It is most likely a word invented by Strindberg. Most translators change it to a more conventional "burning hot" but Paul loves the insight it gives into the character of the confectioner. He describes the weather in terms that relate to him. The hot weather rots the Confectioner's fruits and makes it so he can't make his jelly. His frustration with the weather isn't just that he is sweaty — he can't do his job and he's losing money. While "burning hot" may be easier to say, Paul understands that "rotting warm" actually gives the actor more information and more to play. Paul is always in tune with clues that a playwright gives an actor and works hard to retain those particular hints in his translation. That is what makes these translations simultaneously faithful and actable — a real gift to theater makers and scholars everywhere.

A Dream Becomes a Reality

About eight years ago, I started a program called The Hidden Classics Reading Series — a program devoted to giving readings to worthy classics that are rarely seen on our stages. Its name is a nod to Strindberg's *The Ghost Sonata*:

The sun I saw, or so it seemed
I gazed upon the Hidden One;
And all his work was human joy,
Blessed is he who goodness does.
Since wrathful deeds which you have done
Cannot be cured with hate and strife;
Comfort those you have distressed
And with your goodness have you healed.
No one fears who's not done wrong;
Goodness is the innocent's crown.

The plan was to do plays by a wide variety of authors but my commitment from the beginning was to do one Chamber Play each year and to commission Paul to translate the three plays he hadn't yet translated (he had already translated *The Pelican* for his production in Toronto and *The Ghost Sonata* for a production in San Diego). Then I thought that at the end we could somehow do a production of all five in rep.

Thanks to the Barbro Osher Pro Suecia Foundation, we have the resources to not only do all five plays in rep but to do them right. This is the first time that these plays will be performed in rep in any language, including Swedish. This means that audiences have never before had the chance to experience the plays' interlocking themes and ideas first hand. On November 10, 2012, we will be doing our first marathon of all five plays in order. I can't even describe my excitement for this day. Seeing all five plays in a single sitting will be a deep look into Strindberg's work unlike anything anyone has experienced before. We at Cutting Ball are so grateful to Paul for these wonderful translations and to Mrs. Osher for the support to make them possible.

The Chamber Plays: Common Themes

All five of the Chamber Plays feature themes that obsessed Strindberg throughout his career as well as ideas that especially concerned him at the end of his life: jealousy, settling accounts, reconciling with life, clinging to memories and exacting revenge. Another idea particular to Strindberg is the notion that there are testing powers all around us putting us through life's trials and seeing whether we pass. All the plays deal with the idea of language not as a means of communication but rather as a means of concealing true thoughts from one another. A poignant motif going through The Chamber Plays is an old man longing to be reconnected to a child he hasn't seen in years. This is something that Strindberg was experiencing at the end of his life when his contact with the children of his three marriages was minimal. Another important idea is the failure of justice in a system in which two false witnesses constitute full proof and one true witness is thrown out. Strindberg seems to prefer personal vendettas and revenges to the legal system. The goddess of divine retribution, Nemesis, seems to hover over all of the plays with each one working out the proper balance of vengeance, righteousness and justice. At the same time, each one ends with a sense of transcendence and reconciliation.

There are character types that track through the five plays. Each play but *The Pelican* features an old man at the center and in *The Pelican* — the family's patriarch has just died and his portrait hangs on the mantle. It is easy to read this as the same semi-autobiographical character from Strindberg's autobiographical novels. The plays all have a woman whose faithfulness is questioned. There are young couples, idealistic students, wise old women, and a host of comical townspeople much like the characters Strindberg satirized in his novels.

Music is an important aspect of the plays with Strindberg often specifying the pieces that are being played during different parts of the drama. All of the senses are evoked in Strindberg's writing. The plays are full of smells and tastes, sights and sounds. Hans-Goran Ekman's excellent book *Strindberg and the Five Senses* gives great insights into how the senses contribute to these plays. What is exciting for us has been seeing how these ideas play out differently in each play and how even the style from play to play is different.

Storm – Opus 1

Storm is a play about memory. An old man who left his young wife and child five years ago has created a shrine to them on his mantle. He wants to live out his last years in peace with treasured memories. That peace is shattered when his wife and her new husband move upstairs dragging the old man into their family drama and all the jealousy and strife that comes with dealing with people in the flesh.

The dramaturgy of *Storm* has a meandering, leisurely quality. It has a beautiful, gentle flow but not a strong drive. It feels like we are hearing snatches of everyday conversations without realizing their significance until they are all put together. As in all the Chamber Plays, there are strange coincidences that feel like the characters' destinies are being pulled by an unseen hand, but here the pull is gentle and the revelations are subtle. The characters take strolls and play chess and the plot moves in a similar fashion. The play is very much like the hot summer storm of the title — it blows in and then passes as quickly as it came.

BURNED HOUSE – OPUS 2

Burned House on the other hand is a play of utter destruction and revenge. Unlike the troubled peace of the old man in *Storm*, here characters are ruined utterly — fortunes dashed, marriages ruined, reputations tarnished, and a young man lands in jail. A Stranger comes back to his childhood home after being away for decades only to find it burned to the ground. As the mystery of the burned house is being solved, terrible secrets about the old man's family and the people in the town are brought to light in ways that mean that life will never be the same.

Here the play centers around the burned house. The play moves in the same way the investigation into the rubble does, layers and layers get peeled back and dirty, ashen secrets are revealed. The stories and coincidences in the play are shocking, wild and convoluted. In *Storm*, the small apartment building in which the play takes place is called, "The Quiet House." In *Burned House*, the neighborhood in which the house burned is called "The Morass." These nicknames aptly sum up the different tones of the plays.

THE GHOST SONATA – OPUS 3

The three scenes of *The Ghost Sonata* have three distinctively different tones. The first scene takes place on a street outside a beautiful apartment building. The Student has just come from saving people from a burning house down the street (for our cycle of plays, a nice connection to *Burned House* which directly precedes *The Ghost Sonata* in the order of composition). He gets drawn into the plot by an old man in a wheelchair and he follows a strange set of occurrences and opportunities that lead him closer to his object of desire in much the same way as Arthur Schnitzler's *Dream Story* (or on the movie that the story inspired: *Eyes Wide Shut*). This scene is like a mysterious trail, or Ariadne's thread, following tiny details and odd coincidences from the past to gain access into the building.

The second scene features a "ghost supper" in the Round Room of the apartment featuring one of the strangest cast of characters assembled on a single stage: a mummy who thinks she's a parrot, a rich noble Colonel who's neither rich, noble, nor a Colonel, and a former fiancée who no longer recognizes her betrothed. The action of the scene is a kind of vengeance exacted by stripping one's enemy down in the most degrading and humiliating ways possible. It is a nasty, mean, cold blooded scene that is just ruthless.

In stark contrast to the second scene, the third scene takes place in the Hyacinth Room which is full of flowers and has a beautiful young girl with a harp. The student and the young girl speak in a kind of poetic language that we haven't heard until now. It is all about the language of flowers and shows Strindberg's strong affinity to botany and the symbols of flowers. It seems like paradise and many have interpreted the three scenes as Strindberg's inferno, purgatorio, and paradiso, but this is Strindberg, not Dante, and here even paradise is corrupted. As the Student and the Girl talk, the Student's illusions are shattered and the scene ends with his tirade against the dishonesty of the world and then with her death.

The Ghost Sonata is a progress from outside on the street, to the room in the apartment where guests are received, to the inner sanctum of the apartment where the beautiful and fragrant hyacinths are meant to protect the girl from the offensive sights and smells from the outside. It is a trip down the rabbit hole where nothing is as it seems.

THE PELICAN – OPUS 4

The Pelican is a claustrophobic play that takes place in a sitting room with a desk, rocking chair, chaise lounge and the pungent smell of the corpse that has just been taken to the cemetery. Unlike *The Ghost Sonata*, *The Pelican* stays in one place. It is the kind of play most of us expect when we hear the term "chamber play" and feel that means it must take place in a single room — a chamber. *The Pelican* is about a family that just lost its patriarch. The father's funeral was followed hard upon by the daughter's wedding to the son-in-law. It turns out that the Mother and the Son-in-Law have a secret alliance and are scheming to get the father's inheritance away from his son and daughter. Eventually the son and daughter wake up from their sleepwalking and realize the dishonesty that surrounds them and get their revenge.

The Pelican is a tightly wound drama. It is in many ways the modern chamber version of *Hamlet* and *Electra* — a father murdered by the mother and her lover and the children needing to know where their loyalties lie and what revenge to take. How Strindberg is able to encapsulate these two major dramas in an hour-long play in a tiny room is quite remarkable. Like *Burned House* and *Ghost Sonata*, terrible secrets are reveled, but here it is less of a stripping away and more like a downward spiral. The secrets are revealed in scraps and pieces, with slips of the tongue and half-told stories. It take time to piece it all together. What starts as the most ordinary of the five chamber plays (a mother and a maid in a sitting room), ends in the most extraordinarily dramatic way — with the house burning down. This fire, however, is as purifying as destructive and it leads to the children's reconciliation with the mother after death.

THE BLACK GLOVE – OPUS 5

The Black Glove is the most cheerful and redemptive of the five plays. It takes place at Christmas and owes a simultaneous debt to Goethe's *Faust* and Dickens's *A Christmas Carol* (only Strindberg could find a way how to join these two disparate influences). This play was written after Strindberg had moved into a new kind of apartment building that had many rooms and all kinds of newly developed modern conveniences — the telephone, elevator, and electric lights throughout the house. Strindberg saw it as a modern tower of Babel where disparate souls were joined under one roof who didn't know each other but had connected destinies.

He sets the play in an apartment building and has five scenes in various locations: a vestibule, an entryway, the caretaker's basement, the old man's attic, and the child's room on the third floor. He seems to be tracking all the lives in the building at the same time: the vain young wife and her child, the caretaker, the scholarly old man, the wise old woman, the helpful caretaker, and the maids. In addition to the real characters in the play, there are also a Christmas Angel and a Yule-Tomte (a kind of mischievous spirit charged with protecting a house who later became associated with Christmas). The Angel and the Tomte are able to swoop from room to room and follow the destinies of the building's inhabitants.

The play begins with the old man finding a black glove in the vestibule. The glove contains a ring that Ellen has been accused of stealing. As a punishment for this false accusation, the Angel instructs the Tomte to steal the Young Wife's Child only to be returned to her on Christmas, to teach her an important lesson. The Old Man gives the glove to the Caretaker who loses it, gets it back from the Old Woman, and then loses it again to the Tomte who gives it back to the Old Man who then ultimately gives it to Ellen the maid who finds the ring inside. The passing of the glove from person to person highlights the many ways their destinies are interwoven. The Old Man works tirelessly in the attic to find the meaning of life. It's a dark night of the soul in which the Tomte convinces him to burn all his papers and books. The only thing he keeps is a box of memories which reminds him of the wife and daughter he has left behind. It turns out that the young wife is his very daughter, whose glove he had found, but he dies before being able to reunite with her. The young wife begs Ellen to forgive her for accusing her of stealing the ring and performs the final services on her long lost father in the attic. For this she is rewarded with the return of her child and the Tomte blows her a kiss in the spirit of Chirstmas.

This strange and wonderful play has many different styles running through it. Some scenes are in verse, some are mimed, others are simple, natural and humorous. It is a far more contemplative play than the other Chamber Plays and is the most cheerful and redemptive. It is a tour-de-force displaying all the different aspects of Strindberg's dramaturgy he had developed over the years: realism, fantasy, dream-visions, sleepwalking, casual conversation, and beautiful poetry. It is a fitting end to the chamber plays that together are such a magnificent demonstration of theatrical style and power.

THE ROAD AHEAD

I write this in the middle of our summer workshop in preparation for our fall full productions of these plays in repertory. Finding a design strategy and performance style that both unifies these plays and highlights their extraordinary differences has been a remarkable challenge. It reminds me of the challenge I took sixteen years ago of directing Strindberg's last play, *The Great Highway*, which many considered to be unproduceable. Whether it was a success or a failure, it started a lifelong love of Strindberg which I value most highly.

Likewise, whether our upcoming journey succeeds or fails, we have already gained one enormous success — these magnificent translations by Paul Walsh. I hope you enjoy reading these plays that we prize enough to dedicate a healthy chunk of our lives to realizing. They are extraordinary.

Rob Melrose
San Francisco
August 2012

Storm

Opus 1 of the Chamber Plays (1907)

Storm

Characters

THE GENTLEMAN, A retired official.
THE BROTHER, Consul.
CONFECTIONER STARCK.
ANGES, Starck's daughter.
LOUISE, The Gentleman's maid.
GERDA, The Gentleman's former wife.
FISCHER, Gerda's new husband.
THE ICEMAN.
THE POSTMAN.
THE LAMPLIGHER.
[THE DELIVERY MAN]

1.

The façade of a modern brick apartment building covered in yellow stucco. The foundations are granite and the window ledges and other ornamentation are sandstone. In the middle of the foundations is an entryway into the courtyard and to the basement confectionary shop. On the right, the façade ends at a corner beyond which part of the courtyard can be seen bordered in rambling roses and other flowers. At the corner is a letter box. The great windows on the ground floor are open. Four of these belong to an elegantly furnished dining room. The four windows of the second floor apartment are covered with red shades lit from behind.

A sidewalk and the trees of the avenue can be seen in front of the building. In the foreground are a green bench and a gas lamp.

The CONFECTIONER brings a chair out to the sidewalk and sits.

The GENTLEMAN can be seen sitting at the dining room table on the ground floor. Behind him is a Majolica-tile stove. On the mantel is a large photograph between two candle sticks and flower vases. A young woman dressed in light colors serves the final *course.*

Outside, the BROTHER enters from the left and knocks with his cane on the windowpane.

BROTHER Almost finished?

GENTLEMAN I'll be right out.

BROTHER *(Greeting the CONFECTIONER)* Good evening, Mr. Starck. Still warm out . . .

The BROTHER sits on the bench.

CONFECTIONER Good evening, Consul. It's rotting warm and we've been making jam all day . . .

BROTHER Oh really . . . a good year for the fruit?

CONFECTIONER Decent enough. The spring was cool, but the summer unbearable warm. Those of us who stayed here in town, we've felt it . . .

BROTHER I came in from the countryside yesterday. When the evenings get dark, one starts to long for . . .

CONFECTIONER Neither me nor the wife have been beyond the city limits, business has been at a standstill, but you have to be on the job preparing for winter. First there's strawberries then cherries, then raspberries and gooseberries, melons, and the whole fall harvest . . .

BROTHER Tell me something, Mr. Starck. Are they planning to sell the building here?

CONFECTIONER Not that I've heard.

BROTHER Do many people live here?

CONFECTIONER Ten families, I believe, if you count the back courtyard. But people don't know each other. There's unusually little gossip here. It seems more like people hide themselves. I've lived here ten years. The first two years a couple lived in the back courtyard that kept quiet all day long. But at night wagons would come in and fetch something. It was the end of the second year I found out finally they were running a nursing home and what they fetched was corpses.

BROTHER Chilling.

CONFECTIONER It's called the quiet house.

BROTHER Yes, people talk pretty little here.

CONFECTIONER Still, there's been dramas . . .

BROTHER Tell me, Mr. Starck, who lives on the second floor above my brother?

CONFECTIONER Yes, up there where the red shades are lit up. The tenant died there during the summer and the place stood empty for a month, and then eight days ago a couple moved in who I've never seen . . . Don't know their name even. Don't believe they've gone out once. Why do you ask?

BROTHER Well . . . I don't know. Those red shades look like stage curtains behind which someone's rehearsing bloody dramas . . . my imagination. That palm tree looks like an iron funeral spray casting shadows on the shades . . . now if we could just see some figures . . .

CONFECTIONER I've seen a whole crowd up there, but only later, at night!

BROTHER Ladies or gentlemen?

CONFECTIONER Both kinds probably ... but I should get back down to my pots . . .

> *The CONFECTIONER goes in through the door. The GENTLEMAN in the dining room has stood up and lit a cigar. He talks to his BROTHER through the window.*

GENTLEMAN I'm almost ready — Louise just has to sew a button on my glove.

BROTHER Are you thinking of going down into town then?

GENTLEMAN Maybe we could walk in that direction . . . who were you talking to?

BROTHER Just the Confectioner...

GENTLEMAN Yes, he's a decent man: my only company here during the summer...

BROTHER Have you really stayed in every evening, never been out?

GENTLEMAN Never! The light evenings make me shy. It must be beautiful in the countryside, but here in town it seems against the proper order of things, almost uncanny. Once they've started lighting the lamps again, I begin to calm down. I can go out for my evening walk. That tires me out and I sleep better...

> *LOUISE delivers the glove.*

Thank you, my child... you can leave the windows open, there're no mosquitoes... now I'm ready!

> *In a moment, the GENTLEMAN is seen coming out from the courtyard. He puts a letter in the letter box and sits on the bench next to his brother.*

BROTHER So tell me, why do you stay in town when you could go out to the country?

GENTLEMAN I don't know. I've become immobilized. I'm bound to my apartment by memories... I feel calm and protected in there. Only in there. It's interesting to see one's home from the outside. I pretend it's someone else wandering in there... Just think, I've wandered around in there for ten years...

BROTHER Is it ten years already?

GENTLEMAN Yes, time passes quickly, once it's past, but while its passing it drags on... The house was new back then. I watched them put the parquet floor in the sitting room, watched them paint the wooden panels and doors, and she got to choose the wallpaper. It's still there... yes, that was it. The Confectioner and I are the oldest in the building, and he's had his bouts with destiny too... He's the kind of man who never gets a lucky break, always ends up in some kind of tangle. It's like I've lived his life and borne his burdens alongside my own.

BROTHER Does he drink then?

GENTLEMAN No, he doesn't neglect things but he has no drive . . . Still, we know the chronicle of the house, he and I. They arrive in wedding carriages here and depart in hearses. And that letter box: it's held its share of confidences . . .

BROTHER You had a death here in the middle of summer?

GENTLEMAN Typhoid. A bank clerk. And then the apartment sat empty for a month. First the casket came out, then the widow and children, and finally the furniture . . .

BROTHER On the second floor?

GENTLEMAN There above mine, where the lights are on, at the newcomers whom I haven't met yet.

BROTHER And you've not seen them either?

GENTLEMAN I never ask about the other tenants. What presents itself of its own free will I accept, without misusing it or getting involved. I'm protective of the peace and quiet of old age . . .

BROTHER Ah yes, the peace and quiet of old age. I think it's nice being old. There's not so much left on the record.

GENTLEMAN Yes it is nice. I'm closing out my accounts with life and with people. I've even begun to pack for the trip. Being alone is so-so, but when no one has a claim on you, you've won a kind of freedom: freedom to come and go, to think and act, to eat and sleep whatever or whenever you want.

> *One of the blinds is drawn up in the upper apartment, but only a little, so one can see a woman's dress, then the blind falls quickly again.*

BROTHER They're starting to move around up there. Did you see?

GENTLEMAN Yes, it's all so secretive, but it's worst at night. Sometimes there's music, but always bad music. Sometimes I could swear they're playing cards, and then after midnight carriages arrive to pick people up . . . I never complain about the other tenants; they'd just take revenge and nothing would come of it . . . It's best not to know anything.

> *A bareheaded man in evening dress comes out from the courtyard,*

puts a large packet of mail in the letter box, then vanishes.

BROTHER That was quite a lot mail he had.

GENTLEMAN It looked like circulars.

BROTHER But who was he?

GENTLEMAN It must have been the tenant who lives above me . . .

BROTHER That was him? What kind of man did he look like, do you think?

GENTLEMAN I don't know. A musician, a conductor, comic opera bordering on vaudeville, a card shark, a gigolo, a little of everything . . .

BROTHER With such white skin he should have had black hair, but it was brown—so, either it's dyed or a toupee; evening dress at home suggests a lack of wardrobe and the way his hands moved when he put his mail in the letter box looked like he was shuffling and dealing . . .

A waltz is heard very faintly from the upper apartment.

Always waltzes, maybe they're running a dancing school, but it's always the same waltz. What's it called?

GENTLEMAN If memory serves . . . it's "Pluie d'Or"[1] . . . I know it by heart . . .

BROTHER Was it played around the house?

GENTLEMAN Yes, that one and the Alcazar . . .

LOUISE is seen in the dining room putting the dried stemware away in the sideboard.

BROTHER Are you still satisfied with Louise?

GENTLEMAN Very.

BROTHER She's not planning to get married?

GENTLEMAN Not that I know of.

BROTHER No fiancé in sight?

GENTLEMAN Why do you ask that?

BROTHER Perhaps you're considering it?

GENTLEMAN Me? No thank you. When I got married the last time I wasn't too old. We had a child right away. But now I am, and now I want to grow old in peace . . . do you think I want an overlord in my own home? To hand over my life, my honor, and my goods?

BROTHER Your life and your goods you can keep . . .

GENTLEMAN Is there something wrong with my honor then?

BROTHER Don't you know?

GENTLEMAN What are you saying?

BROTHER She murdered your honor when she left . . .

GENTLEMAN You mean I've been walking around a murder victim for five years without knowing it?

BROTHER Have you really not known?

GENTLEMAN No, but let me tell you in a few words what really happened . . . when I got married again at age fifty to a relatively young girl whose heart I had won and who gave me her hand without fear or compulsion, I promised that when my age became a burden to her youth, I'd go my way, give her back her freedom. Then the child came, in the proper course of time, and neither of us wanted any more. And my daughter began to grow apart from me, and I felt superfluous, so I walked out, or rather I took a boat since we were on an island, and after that the story was over. I had kept my promise, and saved my honor. What more?

BROTHER Yes, but she wanted to be the one to leave, felt her honor had been attacked, and so she murdered yours, with quiet accusations that you were never allowed to hear.

GENTLEMAN Did she accuse herself too?

BROTHER No, she had no grounds.

GENTLEMAN Well, then, there's no danger.

BROTHER Have you heard anything about her fate, and the child's, since then?

GENTLEMAN I wish to know nothing! After I had lived through all the phases of emptiness, I considered the affair buried, and since only beautiful memories remained in this apartment, I stayed. But thank you for this valuable piece of information.

BROTHER Which?

GENTLEMAN That she had nothing to accuse herself of, since that would have been an accusation against me . . .

BROTHER I believe you're living a willful lie.

GENTLEMAN Then let me live it, brother. A clear conscience, relatively clear, has always been like a diving suit to me. It lets me go down into the deeps without suffocating. *(He stands)* At least I came out of it with my life! And now it's past! Shall we go for a little walk on the avenue?

BROTHER We could do that, and watch them light the street lamps.

GENTLEMAN Won't there be moonlight this evening, the August moon?

BROTHER I believe the moon will be full . . .

GENTLEMAN *(Speaking through the window)* Louise, will you hand me my cane please? The light summer one, just to hold in my hand.

LOUISE *(Handing out a walking stick)* Here you are, sir.

GENTLEMAN Thank you, child. You can put the lights out in the dining room, if you don't have anything more to do there . . . we'll be out a while, can't say how long . . .

> The GENTLEMAN and the BROTHER go out to the left. LOUISE stands in the window. The CONFECTIONER comes out through his door.

CONFECTIONER Good evening, miss. It's still a bit warm . . . Have your gentlemen gone out?

LOUISE They've gone for a little walk on the avenue . . . It's the first evening he's been out all summer.

CONFECTIONER We old folks love the dusk, it covers so many faults, in us and others . . . did you know my wife's going blind but doesn't want an operation: There's nothing to see, she says. And sometimes she wishes she were deaf too.

LOUISE It can seem that way sometimes.

CONFECTIONER You lead a quiet, beautiful life in there, prosperous and without worries. I've never heard a raised voice or a slammed door. Maybe a bit too quiet for a young girl like you?

LOUISE Goodness no, I love the quiet and the pleasant, dignified reserve of not saying everything you think, and behaving like it's a responsibility to overlook the insignificant little complaints of life . . .

CONFECTIONER You never have visitors?

LOUISE No, only the Consul. I've never seen such love between brothers.

CONFECTIONER Which of them is actually the elder?

LOUISE I can't say . . . if a year separates them or a couple, or if they're twins, I don't know, since they treat each other with such respect. As if each were the older brother.

* * *

AGNES comes out and tries to sneak by the CONFECTIONER.

CONFECTIONER Where do you think you're going, my girl?

AGNES I'm just going out for a little walk.

CONFECTIONER All right then, but come right back.

AGNES goes.

CONFECTIONER Do you think he grieves his loved ones still?

LOUISE He doesn't grieve, doesn't miss them either since he doesn't wish for them back. But he lives with them in his memory where he only accepts what's beautiful . . .

CONFECTIONER But the daughter's fate worries him sometimes . . .

LOUISE Yes, he must fear that if the mother remarries much will depend on who the stepfather is . . .

CONFECTIONER People have said that at the start the wife refused all support, but then after five years she sent a lawyer with a long accounting for several thousand . . .

LOUISE *(Turning away)* I don't know anything about it . . .

CONFECTIONER Anyway, I do believe the wife is most beautiful in his memory . . .

DELIVERY MAN *(Entering with a basket of wine bottles)* Pardon me, does Mr. Fischer live here?

LOUISE Mr. Fischer? Not that I know of.

CONFECTIONER Maybe the one upstairs is Fischer? Ring the bell for the second floor, at the corner.

DELIVERY MAN *(Goes into the courtyard)* Second floor, thanks very much.

* * *

LOUISE Now it'll be another sleepless night if they're bringing up bottles.

CONFECTIONER What kind of people are they? How come you never see them?

LOUISE They always go out the back way. I've never seen them. But I hear them!

CONFECTIONER I've heard it too. Doors slam, corks pop, and maybe other things slam and pop too . . .

LOUISE They never open the windows, in this heat. They must be from the south . . . Look, lightning! One, two, three . . . it must be heat lighting. There's no thunder.

A VOICE *(From down below)* Starck darling, come down and help with the syrup.

CONFECTIONER I'm coming old girl. — You see, we're in the middle of making jam . . . I'm coming, I'm coming . . .

> *The CONFECTIONER goes down to his shop.*

* * *

> LOUISE *remains standing at the window.*

* * *

BROTHER *(Entering slowly from the right)* Hasn't my brother come back?

LOUISE No, Herr Consul.

BROTHER He stopped to make a telephone call, and I went on ahead. Anyway, he'll be back again in a minute . . . Well, what is this? *(He bends down and picks up a postcard)* The Boston Club after midnight . . . The Fischers — who are the Fischers? Do you know, Louise?

LOUISE There was a man here with wine looking for the Fischers, the second floor.

BROTHER Second floor, Fischers! Red window shades that glow like a cigar at night. I do believe you have some bad company in the house!

LOUISE What is the Boston Club?

BROTHER It could be something completely innocent, of course, though in this case I doubt it . . . But this post card? He dropped it a minute ago. I'll put it in the letter box . . . Fischer? I've heard that name before, in connection with something I've forgotten . . . Miss Louise, may I ask you a question? Has my brother every spoken about — — — the past?

LOUISE Never with me.

BROTHER Miss Louise . . . may I ask . . .

LOUISE Excuse me, the evening milk delivery is here and I have to take it in . . .

> *LOUISE takes her leave. The MILKMAID can be seen entering on the right and going into the courtyard.*

* * *

CONFECTIONER *(Out again, takes off his white hat, panting)* In and out like a badger in his hole . . . It's absolutely terrible down there by the stove . . . and no evening breeze at all.

BROTHER There'll be rain, since there's lightning . . . It isn't all that pleasant in town, but up here it's calm. Never the noise of a wagon, much less a streetcar. It's like being out in the country.

CONFECTIONER It's calm alright, but too calm for business. I can do my job, but I'm a terrible salesman, always have been, and can't seem to learn, or maybe it's something else . . . Maybe I don't have the knack. If a customer treats me like a cheat, I get intimidated and then I get mad. But I can't quite manage to get really upset these days. It wears thin, everything wears thin.

BROTHER Why don't you go work for someone else then?

CONFECTIONER No one will have me.

BROTHER Have you tried?

CONFECTIONER What good would it do?

BROTHER I see.

> *From the upper apartment, a long, drawn-out cry is heard.*

CONFECTIONER What in heaven's name are they doing up there? Killing each other?

BROTHER I don't like these new strangers in the house. It's like a red thundercloud hanging over us. What kind of people are they? Where do they come from? What do they want here?

CONFECTIONER It's dangerous to root around in others' business. You only get mixed up in it . . .

BROTHER Don't you know anything about them?

CONFECTIONER Not a thing . . .

BROTHER There's another scream in the stairwell . . .

CONFECTIONER *(Goes in, shaken)* I want nothing to do with this . . .

* * *

> GERDA, *the* GENTLEMAN's *former wife, comes out through the courtyard, bareheaded with her hair down, upset. The* BROTHER *goes over to her. They recognize each other. She recoils.*

BROTHER So it is you.

GERDA Yes, it is I.

BROTHER How did you end up here? Why can't you leave my brother in peace?

GERDA *(Crazed)* They gave me the wrong tenants' list. I thought he had moved. I didn't do this . . .

BROTHER Don't be afraid of me. You shouldn't be afraid of me, Gerda . . . Can I help you? What's going on up there?

GERDA He hit me!

BROTHER Is your little girl with you?

GERDA Yes.

BROTHER So she has a stepfather?

GERDA Yes.

BROTHER Put up your hair and calm down, and I'll try to sort this out, but spare my brother . . .

GERDA He hates me?

BROTHER No, don't you see how he looks after your flowers in the flowerboxes. He carried the dirt here himself, remember, in a basket.

Do you recognize your blue gentians and mignonettes, your roses — Malmaison and Merveille de Lyon, which he grafted himself. Do you see how he's guarded your memory and your daughter's?

GERDA Where is he now?

BROTHER He's out for a walk on the avenue. He'll be back soon with the evening paper. He'll come in from that direction and go through the courtyard. Then he'll sit in the dining room and read. Stay still and he won't notice you. — But you should go back up again to your . . .

GERDA I can't. I can't go back to that man . . .

BROTHER Who is he, and what?

GERDA He . . . he was a singer.

BROTHER And now? A conman.

GERDA Yes.

BROTHER A gambling house?

GERDA Yes.

BROTHER And the child? A song bird in a cage?

GERDA Don't say that.

BROTHER It is terrible.

GERDA You're making too much of it.

BROTHER Towards filth one should be charming, but anything that's good and moral one should drag down. Why did you defile his honor? And why did you trick me into helping you do it? Obviously I was childish enough to believe you, and I swore to your unjust case against him.

GERDA You forget, he was too old.

BROTHER No, he wasn't then, since you two had a child almost immediately: when he proposed and asked you if you would have a child with him, he promised to give you your freedom when he'd fulfilled his pledge and his age began to weigh on you.

GERDA He abandoned me and that was an insult — .

BROTHER Not for you. Your youth shielded you from shame . . .

GERDA How dare he let me go.

BROTHER Why? Why did you want him disgraced?

GERDA Somebody had to be.

BROTHER Your thinking is so strange. So you murdered him and deceived me at the same time. How are we ever going to make things right?

GERDA If things are made right for him it will be at my cost.

BROTHER I can't follow your thoughts. They always turn to hate. Then how about if we forget trying to make things right for him and think instead about saving his daughter? What can we do?

GERDA She's my child. The law gave me custody, and my husband is her father . . .

BROTHER Now you're making too much of this. You're getting wild and coarse . . . Quiet, here he comes.

> *The GENTLEMAN enters from the left with a newspaper in his hand and goes, deep in thought, into the courtyard, while the BROTHER and GERDA stand still, hidden in the shadows. When he has gone, the BROTHER and GERDA come out of the shadows. The GENTLEMAN appears sitting down in his dining room with the newspaper.*

GERDA It was him.

BROTHER Come over here and look at your home. How he's left everything just as it was, arranged to your taste. — Don't be afraid, he can't see us out here in the dark — the light blinds him, you see.

GERDA Just think how he lied to me . . .

BROTHER What do you mean?

GERDA He's not aged at all. He just got tired of me. That's all it was. Look at his collar and cravat, they're the latest fashion. I'm certain he has a lover.

BROTHER You can see her portrait on the mantelpiece between the candle sticks.

GERDA It's me and the child. Does he still love me?

BROTHER Your memory.

GERDA How strange.

> *The GENTLEMAN looks up, listening, and stares out through the window.*

GERDA He's looking at us.

BROTHER Stand still.

GERDA He's staring me right in the eye.

BROTHER Stand still. He doesn't see you.

GERDA He's like a dead man . . .

BROTHER He was murdered.

GERDA Why do you say that.

> *The BROTHER and GERDA are lit by a bright streak of lightning. In the dining room, the GENTLEMAN shudders and rises. GERDA flees around the corner.*

GENTLEMAN Karl Frederik! *(At the window)* Are you alone? — I thought . . . are you really alone?

BROTHER As you see.

GENTLEMAN It's so close and the flowers give me a headache . . . I'll just finish my newspaper . . .

> *The GENTLEMAN returns to his place at the table.*

BROTHER *(At GERDA's side)* Now, back to your apartment. Shall I follow you up?

GERDA Perhaps. But there'll be such a fight.

BROTHER The child must be rescued. And I am an officer of the court.

GERDA Well, for the child's sake. Follow me.

> *They go.*

GENTLEMAN *(From within)* Karl Fredrik! Come play a game of chess. Karl Fredrik!

> *Curtain.*

2.

> *Inside the dining room. In the back, a tile stove; to the left, a door into the pantry; to the right, a door into the hallway. To the left, a buffet with a telephone; to the right, a piano with a clock on it. Doors in the right and left walls.*
>
> *LOUISE enters.*

GENTLEMAN Where'd my brother go?

LOUISE *(Troubled)* He was just outside. He can't have gone far.

GENTLEMAN There's a terrible uproar upstairs. It's as if they were trampling on my head. Now they're pulling out bureau drawers as if they were planning to leave, perhaps run away . . . If only you could play chess.

LOUISE I can a little . . .

GENTLEMAN If you know how the pieces move, the rest takes care of itself . . . Sit down my child.

> *The GENTLEMAN sets up the chess board.*

They're so loud up there the chandelier's shaking . . . And below the confectioner's stoves are being lit . . . I think I will have to move soon.

LOUISE You should do that anyway, I've thought for a long time.

GENTLEMAN Oh?

LOUISE It's not good to sit so long with old memories.

GENTLEMAN And why not? When time has gone, all memories are beautiful.

LOUISE But you could live twenty years more, and that's too long to sit with memories, which only fade, and perhaps some day change colors.

GENTLEMAN You know so much, my child.— Start now, move a pawn. But not the queen's pawn or it will be over in two moves.

LOUISE Then I'll start with the knight . . .

GENTLEMAN Just as dangerous, my dear.

LOUISE Still, I think I'll begin with the knight.

GENTLEMAN Good. Then I'll move my bishop's pawn . . .

> *The CONFECTIONER is seen in the hallway with a tray.*

There's Mr. Starck with some pastries. He's as quiet as a mouse.

> *LOUISE gets up and goes out to the hall, takes the tray and goes into the pantry.*

Well, Mr. Starck. How are things with the old woman?

CONFECTIONER Yes, thank you. It's the eyes as usual.

GENTLEMAN Have you seen my brother?

CONFECTIONER He must be strolling around outside.

GENTLEMAN Has he found someone to walk with?

CONFECTIONER No, I don't think so.

GENTLEMAN It's been a while since you've been here in my home.

CONFECTIONER Nearly ten years

GENTLEMAN When you came with the wedding cake . . . Do things look the same?

CONFECTIONER Exactly the same . . . The palm tree has grown, of course. Yes, exactly the same . . .

GENTLEMAN And it'll stay that way until you come with the funeral cake. After a certain age, nothing changes, everything stays the same. One pushes forward like a sled on a slope.

CONFECTIONER So it is.

GENTLEMAN And in that way it's peaceful . . . No love, no friends, only a little company in the midst of solitude. People become people, without claims on your feelings or sympathies. One gets loose like an old tooth, and then falls out without pain or loss. Take Louise for example. A beautiful young girl. And seeing her I experience a certain satisfaction, like looking at a work of art one has no desire to own. Nothing disturbs our relationship. My brother and I get along like two old gentlemen who never get too close to one another or take advantage of confidences. By keeping things neutral with others, one develops a certain distance, and with distance things go better. In a word, I'm satisfied with old age and its peace and quiet. *(He calls)* Louise!

LOUISE *(Entering through the door on the right, amiable as always)* The laundry's finished, and I have to check it . . .

GENTLEMAN Well, Mr. Starck, won't you sit down and talk a bit? Perhaps a game of chess?

CONFECTIONER I can't be away from my pots, and the ovens have to be lit at eleven . . . Thanks anyway for your kind offer . . .

GENTLEMAN If you happen to see my brother, ask him to come in and keep me company . . .

CONFECTIONER I certainly will . . . I certainly will.

    The CONFECTIONER goes.

* * *

Alone, the Gentleman moves chess pieces for a few seconds, then gets up and wanders around.

GENTLEMAN Louise! Couldn't you skip the laundry for now?

LOUISE *(Looking in through the door on the right)* Not right now. The washer woman is in a hurry. Her husband and children are waiting for her . . .

The GENTLEMAN sits at the table and drums with his fingers. He tries to read the newspaper but tires of it. He lights some matches and blows them out. He looks at the clock. There's a sound in the hallway.

GENTLEMAN Is that you, Karl Fredrik?

* * *

POSTMAN It's just the postman. Forgive me coming in, but the door was open.

GENTLEMAN Is there a letter for me?

POSTMAN Just a postcard.

The POSTMAN leaves the card and goes.

* * *

GENTLEMAN *(Reading the card)* Herr Fischer again! The Boston Club! That's him up there. With the white hands and in evening dress. And to me! The audacity! I have to move out of here — Fischer!

He tears the card into pieces.

Is that you, Karl Frederik?

* * *

ICEMAN It's the iceman.

GENTLEMAN It's good getting ice in this heat. But watch out for the bottles in the cabinet. And lay the ice on its side so I can hear it melt and the drops of water fall — it's my water clock, measuring out the time, the long long time . . . Tell me, where do you get the ice from? — Has he gone? — Everyone goes, home, to hear their own voices and enjoy some company . . . *(Pause)* Is that you, Karl Frederik?

> *Chopin's* Fantasie Impromptu Opus 66[2] *is being played on a piano in the apartment above, but only the first part.*

GENTLEMAN *(Listens, awakens, looks up at the ceiling)* Who's playing? My impromptu?

> *He listens with his hand in front of his eyes. The BROTHER enters from the hallway.*

GENTLEMAN Is that you, Karl Frederik?

> *The music stops abruptly.*

BROTHER It is.

GENTLEMAN Where have you been for so long?

BROTHER I had something I had to take care of. Have you been alone?

GENTLEMAN Of course. Come and play chess.

BROTHER I'd rather talk. And it might do you some good too to hear your own voice.

GENTLEMAN Quite true, but we always fall so quickly into the past.

BROTHER That's how one forgets the present . . .

GENTLEMAN There is no present. All this is nothing: either forward or backward — best forward, for that's where hope lies.

BROTHER *(At the table)* Hope for what?

GENTLEMAN Change.

BROTHER Well. Are you saying you've had enough of the peace and quiet of old age?

GENTLEMAN Perhaps.

BROTHER That means probably. And if you had to choose between solitude and the past . . .

GENTLEMAN No ghosts though.

BROTHER And your memories?

GENTLEMAN They don't haunt me: they're poems I've made out of past realities. But if the dead should return, they would be ghosts.

BROTHER In any case, in your memories, which of the two creates the more beautiful illusion: the woman or the child?

GENTLEMAN Both. I can't separate them. That's why I never sought to keep the child.

BROTHER But was it handled right? Didn't you think about the possibility of a stepfather?

GENTLEMAN I didn't think so far into the future then. But since then I've — reflected — on the matter.

BROTHER A stepfather who mistreated, perhaps even degraded your daughter?

GENTLEMAN Quiet!

BROTHER What do you hear?

GENTLEMAN I thought I heard "the patter of little feet," those small skipping steps in the hall, when she would come looking for me. — It was the child who was the best. To see that little being that nothing frightened, knowing nothing of the deceits of life, with no secrets. I remember her first experience of human malice. She saw a beautiful little baby down in the park, and she ran over with open arms to kiss the unknown infant. The beautiful baby responded to her kindness by biting her on the cheek and then stuck out her tongue. You should have seen my little Anne-Charlotte then: she stood stock still, not because of the pain but because of the horror of seeing the abyss of what's called the human heart open up in front of her. I have seen it once, when behind the most beautiful eyes there was suddenly staring out at me the strangest gaze, like a beast of prey. I was literally so frightened I looked to see if someone else stood behind her face, which was like a mask. But why are we talking about this? Is it the heat and lightning or what?

BROTHER Solitude brings heavy thoughts. You should have company. Spending the summer in town seems to have broken you.

GENTLEMAN Only the past few weeks. The sickness and death upstairs affected me like I was going through it myself. The confectioner's troubles and worries have also become mine. I worry about his income and his wife's eye problems, and his future . . . and now these past few days I've been dreaming every night about little Anne-Charlotte . . . I see her in danger, unknown, lost, without a name. And just before I fall asleep, my hearing gets unbelievably sharp, and I hear her small steps. Once I heard her voice . . .

BROTHER Where is she, then?

GENTLEMAN Yes — .

BROTHER If you were to meet her on the street . . .

GENTLEMAN I imagine I would lose my mind or fall to the ground . . . Once I was out of the country for a long time. And during that time my little sister grew up . . . after several years I came back, and found a young woman at the boat dock who embraced me. I looked with terror into those two eyes boring into mine with the gaze of a stranger and a terrible sense of alarm at not being recognized. "It's me," she kept repeating before I recognized my own sister. That's how I imagine seeing my daughter again would be. Five years at her age can make one unrecognizable. Imagine not recognizing your own child. The same, but a stranger. I'd never survive it. No, I'd rather stick to my little four-year-old there on the Altar to the Home. I don't want any other . . . *(Pause)*

Is that Louise rummaging around in the linen closet? It smells clean. It reminds me . . . yes, the mother in the linen closet, the good fairy who soothes and renews, the housewife with the iron smoothing away the wrinkles . . . the wrinkles.

>   *Pause.*

I have to go in and write a letter. Will you stay? I'll be right back.

>   *The GENTLEMAN goes out to the right.*

* * *

>   *The BROTHER coughs.*

GERDA *(Standing in the hallway door)* Are you . . . *(The clock chimes)* Oh God! That chime. . . I've heard it in my head for ten years. That clock. It never kept good time, but it measured out five long years by the hour, day and night. *(Looking around)* My piano . . . my palms . . . the dining room table. He's cared for it with honor, bright as a shield. My buffet with the knight and Eve with the apple in her basket . . . In the right drawer, furthest back, there was a thermometer . . . *(Pause)* I wonder if it's still there . . . *(Goes to the buffet and pulls out the right drawer)* Yes, there it is.

BROTHER What's that about?

GERDA It became a symbol of impermanence in the end. When we first moved in here, that thermometer never got put up. It should have been outside the window . . . I promised to do it . . . but forgot. He promised to do it, but forgot. We nagged each other, until finally I hid it in this drawer . . . I came to hate the thing, and he did too. Do you know what it means? — Well, no one believed our relationship would last, since we took off our masks at the very beginning and showed our asperities. We lived from the first as if on springs . . . ready to fly off at the slightest notice — that was the thermometer . . . and here it still lies. Up and down, always changing, like the weather. *(She sets it aside and goes to the chessboard)* My chess board. He bought it to wile away the long winter days, before the child came. Who does he play with now?

BROTHER Me.

GERDA Where is he?

BROTHER He went into his room to write a letter.

GERDA Where?

BROTHER *(Pointing to the left)* There.

GERDA *(Drawing away)* And he's lived here for five years?

BROTHER Ten years, five of them alone.

GERDA Doe he love solitude?

BROTHER I believe he's had enough of it.

GERDA Will he throw me out?

BROTHER Try. It's not really much of a risk. He's always courteous.

GERDA This table runner is not something I made . . .

BROTHER Of course you do risk that he will ask about the child.

GERDA But he's going to help me find her again . . .

BROTHER Where do you think Fischer has gone and what does he hope to gain with leaving?

GERDA To get out of this awful neighborhood first; and also to get me to follow him. He's using the girl as a hostage, and also to train her for the ballet. She really has shown a gift for it and she has the disposition.

BROTHER Ballet? Don't let her father hear that. He hates the stage.

GERDA *(Sitting at the chess board, she unconsciously begins arranging the pieces)* The stage. I've been on the stage myself.

BROTHER Have you?

GERDA As an accompanist.

BROTHER Poor Gerda.

GERDA Why do you say that? I loved that life. When I sat here as a prisoner, it wasn't the prison keeper's fault that I wasn't happy, but the prison's.

BROTHER But now you've had enough?

GERDA Now I love calm and solitude . . . and my child above all.

BROTHER Quiet, he's coming.

GERDA *(Getting up as if to flee, but falls back into the chair)* Oh!

BROTHER I'm going to leave you. — Don't think about what you're going to say. It'll happen by itself, like the next move in a chess game.

GERDA I fear his first look most, for in it I'll read if I have changed for the better or for the worse . . . if I've gotten old and ugly . . .

BROTHER *(Exiting to the right)* If he finds you older, he'll be able to approach you. If he finds you just as young, he has no hope. He is simpler than you think. — Now.

> *The GENTLEMAN can be seen walking past the open doorway on the left to the pantry. He has a letter in his hand. He disappears but is seen soon after in the hallway. He goes out.*

BROTHER *(In the doorway at the right)* He's gone to the letter box.

GERDA I'll never get through this. How can I ever beg him for help in this? I have to go! It's too presumptuous.

BROTHER Stay! You know his goodness has no bounds. He will help you, for the child's sake.

GERDA No. No.

BROTHER And only he can help.

* * *

> *Entering quickly from the hallway, the GENTLEMAN nods to GERDA whom, because of his nearsightedness, he mistakes for LOUISE. He goes to the telephone on the buffet, addressing GERDA as he passes.*

GENTLEMAN Done already? Set up the pieces, Louise, and we'll start over from the beginning . . .

> *Caught off-guard, GERDA understands nothing. The GENTLEMAN speaks into the telephone with his back to GERDA.*

Hello — Good evening, is that you mamma? — Yes thanks, just fine. Louise is setting up the chess board, but she's tired out from some trouble earlier. — Yes, it's over now and everything's fine. Nothing important. — It has been warm, hasn't it. The lightning was right over our heads, right over us, but never touched down. False alarm. — What did you say? Fischers. Yes, but it seems they're packing up to leave. — Why is that? I don't know any particulars. — Oh really? Really? — Yes, it leaves at 6:15, the outer passage through the archipelago, and it gets in at, let me see, 8:25. — Did you have a good time then? *(A little laugh)* Yes, he is a hoot when you get him started. What did Maria say about it? — During the summer, you mean? Yes, thank goodness, Louise and

I kept each other company. She has such a steady and good disposition. — Oh yes, she is nice. — No, thank you, none of that . . .

> GERDA *has begun to understand and stands up with a slight sense of dread.*

My eyes? Yes, I've gotten so nearsighted, but like the Confectioner's old girl I just say there's nothing to see. I wish I were a little deaf too. Deaf and blind! The neighbors upstairs make such a racket at night . . . some kind of card den . . . What! Someone's broken in on the line to listen.

> *The* GENTLEMAN *hangs up and calls again.*

* * *

> LOUISE *comes to the hallway door, unseen by the* GENTLEMAN. GERDA *watches her with admiration and hate.* LOUISE *goes out through the door on the right.*

GENTLEMAN Are you there? Just imagine, they break in on the line just to listen. So, tomorrow at 6:15. — Thank you as well. — I certainly will. Goodbye Mamma.

> *The* GENTLEMAN *hangs up.* LOUISE *has left.* GERDA *stands in the middle of the room.*

* * *

> *The* GENTLEMAN *turns around and slowly recognizes* GERDA. *He grabs his heart.*

Oh dear God, is it you? Wasn't it Louise just now?

> GERDA *is silent.*

GENTLEMAN *(Weakly)* How — have you — come here?

GERDA Forgive me, I was in the neighborhood, walking by, and suddenly wanted to see my old home . . . the windows were open . . .

> *Pause.*

GENTLEMAN Are things the same?

GERDA Exactly the same, but something's different. Someone else has been here . . .

GENTLEMAN *(Ill at ease)* Are you satisfied — with your life?

GERDA Well yes, I have just what I wished for.

GENTLEMAN And the child?

GERDA She's growing and happy. She's just fine.

GENTLEMAN Then I'll ask nothing more. — *(Pause)* Do you want something from me. May I be of any service?

GERDA Thank you, but . . . there's nothing I need, now that I know things are going well for you too. *(Pause)* Would you like to see Anne-Charlotte?

>   *Pause.*

GENTLEMAN I don't think so, since you say she's well. — It's so difficult to start over again —. Like repeating a lesson one already knows, even though the teacher doesn't think so — I'm so far away from all that — I was in a completely different place — And I can't tie myself again to the past. It's difficult for me to be impolite, but I'm not going to ask you to sit down — you're another man's wife — and you're not the same person I was separated from —

GERDA Am I so — changed?

GENTLEMAN So strange. Voice, gaze, manner . . .

GERDA Have I aged?

GENTLEMAN I don't know. — They saw that after three years there isn't a single atom left of a person's body — after five years everything has been renewed, and therefore you stand there a different person from the one who suffered here — I can hardly tell you I recognize you, as wildly different as you are. And I suppose it would be the same with my daughter.

GERDA Don't talk like that. I'd rather you were angry.

GENTLEMAN Why should I be angry?

GERDA For all the pain I caused you.

GENTLEMAN Have you? I don't remember.

GERDA Didn't you read the indictment?

GENTLEMAN *(Sitting)* No, I left that to the lawyers.

GERDA And the judgment?

GENTLEMAN I didn't read that either. Since I didn't plan to remarry, I didn't need those papers. *(Pause. GERDA sits)* What did the papers say? That I was too old? *(GERDA nods)* It was only the truth, so it shouldn't embarrass you. I wrote precisely the same thing in my counter-claim and asked that the court give you back your freedom.

GERDA You wrote that . . .

GENTLEMAN I wrote not that I was but that I was becoming too old for you.

GERDA *(Struck)* For me?

GENTLEMAN Yes. — I couldn't say that I was too old when we got married, since then the arrival of the child could have been given an unpleasant interpretation. She was our child, wasn't she?

GERDA You know she was. — But . . .

GENTLEMAN Is your point that I'm supposed to be ashamed of my age? Of course if I tried dancing the Boston or playing cards all night I'd soon be in a wheelchair or on the operating table, and that would be shameful.

GERDA You don't look like . . .

GENTLEMAN Did you think I would die from the divorce? *(GERDA keeps uncomfortably silent.)* There are those who contend that you murdered me. Does it look to you like I've been murdered? *(GERDA is embarrassed.)* They say your friends wrote about me in the weekly papers, but I never saw those papers, and they've been nothing but compost for the past five years. You don't have to torture your conscience for my sake.

GERDA Why did you marry me then?

GENTLEMAN You know full well why a man gets married; and I didn't need to beg for your love, you know that too. And you should remember how we smiled at all those friendly advisers who warned you. — But why you wanted me, I've never been able to figure out . . . When after the wedding ceremony you didn't even look at me but behaved like you were at someone else's wedding, I thought maybe you'd accepted a bet to murder me. All my subordinates hated me like every other director in the business, but they immediately became your friends. As soon as I made an enemy, he became your friend. Which led me to say: "True, there's no need to hate your enemies, but why do you have to *love* mine?" Anyway, when I saw where we stood, I began to pack up, but I wanted a living witness that you were playing with lies, and so I waited for the birth of the child.

GERDA Just think. How could you be so false!

GENTLEMAN I may have been secretive, but I never lied! — You transformed my friends into detectives, and tricked my own brother into betraying me. But what was worse, you raised doubts about your own daughter's legitimate birth with your thoughtless talk.

GERDA I've taken it all back.

GENTLEMAN A word that's taken flight can't be recaptured. The very worst of all was that this false reputation touched the child, who according to her mother was — — — .

GERDA No.

GENTLEMAN Yes. So it is. — You built a whole tower on a foundation of lies, and now that tower of lies is crashing down upon you!

GERDA It's not true.

GENTLEMAN Oh yes. I ran into Anne-Charlotte a bit ago . . .

GERDA Have you met . . . ?

GENTLEMAN We met on the stairs, and she said I was her uncle. Do you know what uncle means? An older friend of the family, and of the mother. And I know that in her school I was taken for her uncle. — What a terrible thing for the child.

GERDA Have you met?

GENTLEMAN Yes, but I didn't need to tell anyone. Haven't I the right to keep quiet? Besides, the meeting was so upsetting that I struck it from my memory, as if it had never existed.

GERDA What can I do to make things right for you?

GENTLEMAN You? You can't make things right. Only I can do that.

They look at each other long and hard.

GENTLEMAN That is to say, things are already made right . . .

Pause.

GERDA Can I not make it up to you? Can I not beg you to forgive? To forget . . .

GENTLEMAN What do you mean?

GERDA Restore, repair . . .

GENTLEMAN Do you mean retie the knot? Begin again? Put you back in my home to lord over me? No thank you. I won't have that.

GERDA How can you speak to me like that!

GENTLEMAN See how it feels.

Pause.

GERDA That's a beautiful table runner you have there. . . .

GENTLEMAN Yes, it is beautiful.

GERDA Where did you get it?

Pause.

* * *

LOUISE is seen at the pantry door with a bill in her hand.

GENTLEMAN *(Turning around)* Is that the bill?

GERDA stands and pulls on her gloves so the buttons smoke.

GENTLEMAN *(Taking out money for the bill)* Eighteen and seventy-five. There we have it.

LOUISE May I have a word with you, sir?

The GENTLEMAN rises and goes to the door where LOUISE whispers something to him.

GENTLEMAN Oh Lord . . . *(LOUISE goes out)* Poor Gerda.

GERDA What do you mean? To make me jealous . . . of your maid?

GENTLEMAN No, that is not what I meant.

GERDA Yes, just like when you said you were too old for me, but not for her. I understand the insult . . . she is beautiful, I don't deny it, for a maid . . .

GENTLEMAN Poor Gerda.

GERDA Why do you say that?

GENTLEMAN Because it's a shame. Jealous of my servant. That makes things right . . .

GERDA Me, jealous . . .

GENTLEMAN Why else would you be raging against my quiet, decent friend?

GERDA "A little more than kin . . ."

GENTLEMAN Oh no, my child, I have resigned myself a long time ago . . . and am satisfied with my solitude . . . *(The telephone rings, the GENTLEMAN answers it)* Mr. Fischer? He's not here. — I see, yes, that is I. — Has he run off? — With whom? Mr. Starck's daughter? Oh, dear God. How old is she? — Eighteen. Only a child.

GERDA I know he's run off. — But with another woman! — Now are you happy?

GENTLEMAN No. I am not happy. Though it does lift my soul to see that there is righteousness in the world. Life goes forward quickly, and now you sit where I sat.

GERDA Her eighteen versus my twenty-nine. — I am old, too old for him.

GENTLEMAN Everything is relative, even age. — But on another topic, where is your child?

GERDA My child. I had forgotten her. My child. Dear God. Help me. He took the child with him. He loved Anne-Charlotte as his own daughter . . . Come with me to the police. Come with me.

GENTLEMAN Me? Now you're asking too much.

GERDA Help me.

GENTLEMAN *(Going to the door on the right)* Karl Frederik, come and call a cab. Go with Gerda down to the police station. — You will, won't you?

* * *

BROTHER *(Entering)* Of course I will. We are human beings, for Christ's sake.

GENTLEMAN Quickly! But don't say anything to Mr. Starck. Everything can still be fixed. Poor man — and poor Gerda. — Hurry!

GERDA *(Looking out the window)* It's beginning to rain. Lend me an umbrella . . . Eighteen years old — only eighteen years old! — Quickly.

She goes out with the BROTHER.

GENTLEMAN The peace of old age! — And my child in the hands of a conman. — Louise! *(LOUISE enters)* Come play chess with me.

LOUISE Has the Consul . . .

GENTLEMAN He's gone off on an errand . . . Is it still raining?

LOUSIE No, it's stopped now.

GENTLEMAN Then I'll go out to cool down. *(Pause)* You are a nice girl and understanding. Did you know the confectioner's daughter?

LOUISE Very little.

GENTLEMAN Was she pretty?

LOUISE Yes.

GENTLEMAN Did you know the couple above us?

LOUISE I've never seen them.

GENTLEMAN Prevarication!

LOUISE I've learned to hold my tongue here in this house.

GENTLEMAN I admit that an adopted deafness can be taken too far and can be dangerous. Keep the tea warm. I'm going out to cool down. — Oh, and one more thing, my child. You've seen what's happening here, but don't ask me anything about it.

LOUISE Me? No, sir, I'm not curious.

GENTLEMAN Thank goodness for that.

> *Curtain.*

3.

> *The façade of the building as in Scene One. Lights are on in the confectionary shop. Lights are also on in the second floor apartment. The windows are open and the shades are pulled up.*

* * *

> *The CONFECTIONER comes out his door.*

GENTLEMAN *(On the green bench)* That was quite a little rain storm we had.

CONFECTIONER A real blessing. There'll be more raspberries . . .

GENTLEMAN Then let me order a couple liters. We've gotten tired of putting up jam ourselves. — It just sits and ferments and molds...

CONFECTIONER Yes, I know what you mean. You have to tend the jam jars like mischievous children. Some even put salicylic acid in, but I don't go along with these new tricks...

GENTLEMAN Salicylic acid. Well, it's a kind of antiseptic — and that could be good...

CONFECTIONER Yes, but you can taste it... and it's a trick...

GENTLEMAN Listen, Mr. Starck, do you have a telephone?

CONFECTIONER No, I don't.

GENTLEMAN Oh? —

CONFECTIONER Why do you ask?

GENTLEMAN Oh, I was just thinking... Sometimes one needs a telephone... orders... important messages...

CONFECTIONER Perhaps so, but sometimes it's good to avoid — messages.

GENTLEMAN Undoubtedly! Undoubtedly! — Yes, I always feel a little twinge in my heart when it rings — one never knows what one will hear... and I want to be left in peace... peace above all.

CONFECTIONER Me too.

GENTLEMAN *(Looking at his watch)* They should be lighting the lamp soon.

CONFECTIONER He must have forgotten us. The avenue's already lit up...

GENTLEMAN Then he'll be along soon. It'll be so nice to see the lamp lit again...

> *The telephone in the dining room rings. The GENTLEMAN gets up, grabs his heart, and tries to listen, but he can't hear the conversation.*

Pause. LOUISE comes out.

GENTLEMAN *(Nervous)* Any news?

LOUISE Unchanged.

GENTLEMAN Was it my brother?

LOUISE No, it was the lady.

GENTLEMAN What did she want?

LOUISE To talk to you.

GENTLEMAN I don't want to. Shall I comfort my executioner? I've done that before, but now I'm tired of it. — Look up there. They've gone out and left the lights burning — an empty room that's still lit up is more terrible than in the dark . . . you see ghosts — *(In a whisper)* And the confectioner's Agnes, do you think he knows anything?

LOUISE It's difficult to say. He never talks about his troubles, nor does anyone else in the quiet house.

GENTLEMAN Do you think we should tell him?

LOUISE For God's sake, no . . .

GENTLEMAN But it's certainly not the first time she's caused him to worry?

LOUISE He never talks about her . . .

GENTLEMAN It's horrible! Will this end soon? *(The telephone rings in the dining room)* Now it's ringing again. Don't go. I don't want to know anything. — My child in such company. A conman and a tramp! — It's endless. Poor Gerda!

LOUISE It's better to know for sure — I'll go in — You must do something, sir.

GENTLEMAN I can't move . . . I can take it, but I can't strike back.

LOUISE But if you try to keep a danger at bay, it forces its way in. And if you don't resist, you're overwhelmed.

GENTLEMAN But if you don't get involved, you stay inaccessible.

LOUISE Inaccessible?

GENTLEMAN Things sort themselves out better if you don't entangle yourself by getting involved. How do they expect me to steer with so many passions blowing! I can't ease their suffering or change their course.

LOUISE But the child?

GENTLEMAN I've relinquished my rights . . . and besides — frankly, it's not my affair — especially now, since she's come and destroyed my beautiful memories. She's whittled away everything beautiful that I had hidden, and there's nothing left.

LOUISE It's a kind of freedom.

GENTLEMAN Look how empty it seems in there. Like after everyone has moved out . . . and up there, like after a fire.

LOUISE Who's that coming?

* * *

AGNES enters, anxious, afraid, but controlling herself and goes to the garden door where the CONFECTIONER sits.

LOUISE *(To the GENTLEMAN)* It's Agnes. What does this mean?

GENTLEMAN Agnes! — Things are beginning to straighten themselves out.

* * *

CONFECTIONER Good evening, child, where have you been?

AGNES I went out for a walk.

CONFECTIONER Mamma asked about you several times.

AGNES Oh? Yes, well, here I am now.

CONFECTIONER Why don't you go down and help her light the little oven, that would be nice of you.

AGNES Is she mad at me?

CONFECTIONER How could she ever be mad at you.

AGNES She can, but she doesn't say anything.

CONFECTIONER That's good then, dear one. You get out of a scolding.

> *AGNES goes in.*

* * *

GENTLEMAN *(To LOUISE)* Does he know or doesn't he?

LOUISE May he live on not knowing . . .

GENTLEMAN But what has happened? A breakup. *(To the CONFECTIONER)* Excuse me, Mr. Starck.

CONFECTIONER What is it?

GENTLEMAN I was just thinking . . . Did you happen to see anyone leave here a bit ago?

CONFECTIONER I believe I saw the iceman and the postman.

GENTLEMAN A-hah.— *(To LOUISE)* Perhaps it was a mistake — perhaps they heard wrong — I can't explain this . . . Perhaps he's a bit crazy. What did she say on the telephone?

LOUISE She wanted to talk to you?

GENTLEMAN How did she sound? Was she upset?

LOUISE Yes.

GENTLEMAN I find it a bit presumptuous to turn to me in such an affair . . .

LOUISE But the child!

GENTLEMAN Imagine meeting my daughter on the stairs and when I asked if she recognized me she called me "uncle" and told me her father was upstairs . . . The stepfather has all the rights — they've sat up there tearing me down and rooting me out . . .

LOUISE A cab's stopping at the corner!

> *The CONFECTIONER goes in.*

GENTLEMAN If only the child doesn't return so I don't have them on my hands again — imagine, hearing my child praising her father, the other one — and the same old story starting again: "Why did you marry me?" — "You know very well; but why did you want me?" — "You know very well" and on and on until the end of the world.

LOUISE It's the consul.

GENTLEMAN How does he seem?

LOUISE He's taking his time.

GENTLEMAN Rehearsing what he's going to say. Does he seem satisfied?

LOUISE More hesitant . . .

GENTLEMAN I see . . . It was always like that. Whenever he came near that woman he betrayed me . . . She could charm everyone, except me. To me she was crude, simple, ugly, dumb, and to everyone else she was refined, loveable, beautiful, intelligent. All that hate my independence woke around me, collected around her in the form of unending sympathy for everything that made me wrong. Through her they sought to control me, influence me, wound me, and in the end kill me.

LOUISE I'm going in to sit by the telephone — This storm will eventually blow over.

GENTLEMAN People can't stand independence. They want others to obey them. All my subordinates, right down to the watchman at work, wanted me to obey them. And when I wouldn't, they called me a despot. The maids in the house wanted me to obey them, to eat warmed up food, and when I wouldn't they set my wife against me. In the end she wanted me to obey the child. Then I walked out, and that led to a conspiracy against the tyrant — which was supposed to be me —. Be careful, Louise, as we detonate the mine out here!

* * *

The BROTHER enters from the left.

GENTLEMAN The results — No details.

BROTHER Can we sit? I'm a little tired . . .

GENTLEMAN It's rained on the bench.

BROTHER But if you've been sitting there, it can't be too dangerous for me.

GENTLEMAN As you wish. — Where's my child?

BROTHER Let me begin from the beginning.

GENTLEMAN Begin!

BROTHER *(Slowly)* When I arrived at the station with Gerda . . . I saw him at the ticket counter with Agnes . . .

GENTLEMAN So, Agnes was with him.

BROTHER Yes, and your child. — Gerda stayed out of it and I went up to them. Just then he handed the tickets to Agnes, but when she saw that they were for third class, she threw them in his face and walked out to a cab.

GENTLEMAN Usch!

BROTHER As I demanded an explanation from him, Gerda hurried forward, took the child, and disappeared in the crowd.

GENTLEMAN What did he say?

BROTHER Well, as you know, as soon as one hears the other side of the story, et cetera.

GENTLEMAN Tell me! — Of course he wasn't as bad as we thought. He also had his side . . .

BROTHER Exactly.

GENTLEMAN I can imagine. But you really can't expect me to sit here and listen to my enemy be praised.

BROTHER No, not praise, but extenuating circumstances.

GENTLEMAN Would you ever listen to me when I explained the true situation? Yes, you listened and responded with disapproving silence, as if I were lying. You were always on the side of what was wrong and you only believed lies, and all this because — you were in love with Gerda. And there was also another motive . . .

BROTHER Don't say anything more now, brother. — You see everything from your own point of view.

GENTLEMAN Do you expect me to see my situation from my enemies' point of view. I can't very well lift my hand against myself.

BROTHER I am not your enemy.

GENTLEMAN Yes, when you befriended those who did me wrong! — — — Where is my child?

BROTHER I don't know.

GENTLEMAN How did things end at the station?

BROTHER He left alone for the south.

GENTLEMAN And the others?

BROTHER Vanished.

GENTLEMAN Then I'll have them lording it over me again. *(Pause)* Did you notice if they followed him?

BROTHER No, he was alone.

GENTLEMAN Then we're rid of him, at least. Number two — Those remaining: mother and child.

BROTHER Why are the lights still on up there in the apartment?

GENTLEMAN Because they forgot to put them out.

BROTHER I'll go up . . .

GENTLEMAN No, don't go. — If only they'd never return! Again, again, forced to repeat every lesson.

BROTHER But the beginning has straightened itself out . . .

GENTLEMAN And the worst remains . . . Do you think they will come back?

BROTHER Not her, she'd have to try to make things right in front of Louise.

GENTLEMAN I'd forgotten that. She actually did me the honor of being jealous! I believe there is righteousness in the world.

BROTHER And when she found out that Agnes was younger.

GENTLEMAN Poor Gerda. But in cases like this, one shouldn't tell others that righteousness exists, a vengeful righteousness . . . for it's not really true that they love righteousness. And one should treat their filth nicely. Oh Nemesis — it's only for others! . . . The telephone's ringing. It sounds like a rattlesnake!

LOUISE can be seen answering the telephone.

* * *

Pause.

* * *

GENTLEMAN *(To LOUISE)* Did the snake strike?

LOUISE *(At the window)* May I speak to you, sir?

GENTLEMAN *(To the window)* Tell me.

LOUISE The lady has gone to her mother's in Dalarna to live there with the child.

GENTLEMAN *(To his brother)* Mother and child to the countryside, in their own home. Now things have straightened themselves out. Oh!

LOUISE And the lady asked me to go up and put the lights out in the apartment.

GENTLEMAN Do it at once, Louise, and pull down the shades so we don't have to see it.

> *LOUISE goes.*

* * *

> *The CONFECTIONER comes out.*

* * *

CONFECTIONER *(Looking up)* I think the storm has passed.

GENTLEMAN It really does seem to have cleared. The moon is shining.

BROTHER It was a blessed rain.

CONFECTIONER Absolutely delightful.

GENTLEMAN Look, there comes the lamplighter at last.

* * *

> *The LAMPLIGHTER lights the street lamp.*

GENTLEMAN The first lamp! Now it's autumn. That's our season, old boys. It's starting to get dark, but with the darkness comes understanding that shines with its own blind light, to keep us from going astray —

> *LOUISE can be seen in the upper window. Immediately afterwards it becomes dark.*

GENTLEMAN *(To LOUISE)* Close the windows and pull down the shades, so the memories will lie down and sleep in peace. The peace of old age. And in the fall, I'll move from this quiet house.

Burned House

Opus 2 of the Chamber Plays (1907)

Burned House

Characters

THE DYER, Rudolf Valström.
THE STRANGER, His Brother, Arvid Valström.
THE MASON, Andersson.
THE OLD WOMAN, His Wife.
THE GARDENER, Gustafsson, the Mason's Brother-in-Law.
ALFRED, His Son.
THE STONECUTTER, Albert Eriksson.
MATILDA, His Daughter.
THE HEARSE-DRIVER, Related to the Stonecutter.
A DETECTIVE.
THE PAINTER, Sjöblom.
MRS. VESTERLUND, Owner of the "Last Nail," previously nurse at the Dyer's.
THE WIFE, The Dyer's Wife.
THE STUDENT.

1.

Upstage left are the walls of a burnt-out one-story house. Wallpaper on the walls and a tile stove. Behind the walls, a garden and orchard in bloom. To the right is an outdoor inn with a wreath on a pole, tables and benches. In the foreground to the left is a pile of salvaged furniture and housewares.

The PAINTER works at the outdoor inn repairing the window frames and listening to every conversation. The MASON digs in the ruins. A DETECTIVE enters.

DETECTIVE Is it out now for sure?

MASON Can't see any smoke anyway.

DETECTIVE Then I'd like to ask you a few more questions. —— *(Pause)* You were born here in the quarter?

MASON Oh yes. Seventy-five years I've lived on this street; and when I wasn't yet born this house was built, my father laid the brick.

DETECTIVE And you know everyone in the quarter?

MASON We all know everyone. There's something peculiar about this street; anyone who comes here once never leaves, at least those who do leave always come back sooner or later, till they're driven out to the graveyard down at the end of the road.

DETECTIVE You have a special name for this quarter then?

MASON We call it the Morass, and everyone hates everyone, mistrusts everyone, slanders everyone, torments everyone . . .

Pause.

DETECTIVE So, the fire broke out at 10:30 last night; was the entry door closed then?

MASON You see, I'm afraid I don't know, since I live in the building next door . . .

DETECTIVE Where'd the fire start?

MASON Up in the attic, where the student lives.

DETECTIVE Was he home?

MASON Na-aw, he was at the theater.

POLICMAN Did he leave a lamp burning then?

MASON You see, I'm afraid I don't know . . .

Pause.

DETECTIVE Is the student related to the owner of the house?

MASON Na-aw, I don't think so. — Are you from the police?

DETECTIVE How come the inn didn't catch fire?

MASON They threw a fire blanket over it and wet it down.

DETECTIVE It's strange the apple trees weren't destroyed by the heat.

MASON The buds had just come out and it'd rained during the day, then they burst out in bloom during the night from the heat, a little early I'd say. If we get a frost, the gardener'll be ruined.

DETECTIVE What is this gardener like?

MASON His name's Gustafsson . . .

DETECTIVE But what's he like?

MASON You listen to me now. I'm seventy-five years old . . . so I don't know anything bad about Gustafsson, and if I did I wouldn't tell you.

>   *Pause.*

DETECTIVE And the owner of the house is named Valström, a dyer, around sixty years old, married . . .

MASON Finish that yourself! I'm not going to let you pump me for any more information.

DETECTIVE Was it arson?

MASON All fires are.

DETECTIVE Who do you suspect then?

MASON Any interested party is always suspected by the insurance company. That's why I've never had insurance.

DETECTIVE Did you find anything digging around?

MASON You can usually find the door keys, since no one has time to take them out with the fire pushing in, except sometimes, there are exceptions when it seems they are taken out . . .

DETECTIVE There was no electric lighting in the house?

MASON Not in this old house, and a good thing too, since now they can't blame it on an electrical short.

DETECTIVE Blame it on? A good thing! — Now just a minute . . .

MASON Are you trying to trap me? Don't do that, or I'll just take it all back.

DETECTIVE Take it all back — you can't.

MASON No?

DETECTIVE Oh, no.

MASON Sure, there's no witness.

DETECTIVE Oh no?

MASON No.

> *The DETECTIVE coughs. The WITNESS enters from the left.*

DETECTIVE Here's a witness.

MASON Tricky!

DETECTIVE You don't have to be seventy-five years old to use your wits. *(To the WITNESS)* Let's continue with the gardener.

> *They exit left.*

MASON Now I've done it. But that's what you get for talking.

> *The OLD WOMAN enters with a lunch bag.*

It's a good thing you're here.

OLD WOMAN Let's sit and have some breakfast and take it easy a spell, you must be hungry after this show, I wonder if your brother-in-law Gustafsson will recover, he'd already seeded the hot beds and was about to start digging up the earth, eat now, there's the painter Sjöblom already starting with his spackling knife, imagine Mrs. Vesterlund dodging the fire like that — Well, Sjöblom, now you have work —

> *MRS. VESTERLUND comes out of the inn.*

Hey there Mrs. Vesterlund, you came out of it pretty well, I must say . . .

MRS. VESTERLUND I wonder who's going to reimburse me for what

I'm losing today, you know there's a big funeral at the graveyard and those are always my best days, I had to take away all the bottles and glasses . . .

OLD WOMAN What's the funeral today? I saw a lot of folks out on the road, and of course they wanted to see the fire too . . .

MRS. VESTERLUND I don't think it was a funeral, they were putting a monument up on the bishop's grave — but the worst is the stonecutter's daughter was supposed to marry the gardener's son, as you know, he's in the store down in town, but now the gardener's lost everything. Isn't that his furniture over there?

OLD WOMAN And the dyer's too, probably, it all came out catawampus. Where is the dyer now?

MRS. VESTERLUND He's giving a statement to the police.

OLD WOMAN Ah-ha, ah-ha . . . And there's my cousin and his hearse, he's always thirsty on his way home . . .

* * *

HEARSE DRIVER Good morning, Malvina, so I hear you lit things up pretty good here last night, looks good too, but you would have done better if you'd gotten yourself a new shack . . .

MRS. VESTERLUND God save us! Who've you been out with now?

HEARSE DRIVER I don't remember what his name was, but there was only the one wagon following, and no wreath on the coffin . . .

MRS. VESTERLUND Well, at least it wasn't one of those they were happy to be rid of . . . if you want something to drink, you'll have to go into the kitchen. I don't have anything ready out here, and Gustafsson's on his way over with his wreaths, since there's something going on out in the graveyard today . . .

HEARSE DRIVER Yes, they're putting up some monument to the bishop, he wrote a lot of books, and collected scurf, was a scurf-collector is what they told me.

MRS. VESTERLUND What does that mean?

HEARSE DRIVER He had a cork board he stuck pins in, with flies on them . . . such things we don't understand . . . but I'm sure it's true . . . I'm going into the kitchen now!

MRS. VESTERLUND Go in the back way then, you'll get a drop.

HEARSE DRIVER But I have to talk to the dye-master before I leave. I left the horses over at my cousin's, the stonecutter, you know. I don't like him, as you also know, but we do business together, I mean I recommend him to the boneyard and I can leave my horses in his garden sometimes; tell me when the dye-master gets here, it was lucky he didn't have his factory here.

> *The HEARSE DRIVER goes to the back of the inn; MRS. VESTERLUND goes through the door. The MASON has finished eating and started digging again.*

* * *

OLD WOMAN Find anything?

MASON Nails, and hinges; all the keys are hanging there in a bunch on the door post . . .

OLD WOMAN Were they hanging there before, or did you collect them up?

MASON They were hanging there from the start, when I arrived.

OLD WOMAN How strange, then someone locked all the doors and took the keys out before the fire started! How strange.

MASON It's a little strange, it is, yes, made it harder to put out the fire and get things out. Ah-huh, ah-huh.

> *Pause.*

OLD WOMAN I worked for the dyer's father, I did, forty years ago, and I knew those folks, both the dyer and his brother who moved to America, though they say he's back; the father was an honest man, but the boys were so-so — Mrs. Vesterlund over there she looked after Rudolf, they could never treat each other brotherly, argued and fought all the time — I've seen it; much has happened here in this house, so much I reckon it was time it got smoked out — Usch, what a house!

The one came and the other one left, and now he's back, and here they die, here they were born, here they married and separated — And the brother Arvid in America was thought dead many years, anyway he never collected his inheritance, but now they say like I said that he's come back again, though nobody's seen him — they talk so much! — Well, there's the dyer back from the police station.

MASON He doesn't look very happy, but who can expect that . . . Who was that student up there in the attic, anyway? They stick together here like plaster and straw.

OLD WOMAN I'm afraid I don't know. He had room and board for tutoring the children.

MASON And the lady of the house too?

OLD WOMAN No, they played whatchacallit tennis and argued; everyone here in the quarter argues and picks at each other — —

MASON When they broke down the student's door, they found it full of hairpins on the floor. All comes out in the light of day, for sure, but first the fire passes through . . .

OLD WOMAN I guess it wasn't the dyer after all, it's Gustafsson . . .

MASON He's always angry, but today he's worse than ever, and now he's going to come and demand his payment after what he's lost in the fire . . .

OLD WOMAN Shush now!

* * *

GARDENER *(Entering with a coal bucket full of wreaths)* Am I going to sell anything today, do you think, so we can eat after such a business?

MASON You weren't insured then?

GARDENER Yes I usually insured the glass in the hot beds, but this year I was going to be clever and used oiled paper instead — imagine being such an ass *(Knocks himself in the head)* — and I won't get a penny for that. Six hundred paper window panes to cut and paste and oil. They always said I was the dumbest of seven kids, such an ass, such a cow! And I went and got drunk last night. Why in hell should I drink last night of all nights when I needed a clear head today. The stonecutter invited me, we're marrying off our kids to each other this evening, but I still should have said no. — Thanks but no. I'm such a cow, who can't say no. And it's just the same when they come to borrow money from me too, I can't say no, poor fool. And I had that cop on me questioning, ensnaring. I should have kept my mouth shut like the painter there, but I can't seem to shut up and so I said some things, and he wrote it all down, and now I'm called to testify.

MASON What did you say for instance?

GARDENER I said I thought — I know it's sick, but that someone had set the fire.

MASON Did you say that?

GARDENER Abuse me, I deserve it, I'm a cow!

MASON Who set it? — Don't worry about the painter, and the old lady's no gossip.

GARDENER Who set it? The student of course, since it started in his room . . .

MASON No, *under* his room!

GARDENER Was it under? And I just said . . . I'm going to end badly; I am; was it *under* his room? You mean underneath? In the kitchen?

MASON No, in the closet; look for yourself there. It was the cook's closet.

GARDENER So it was her!

MASON Don't say that if you don't know.

GARDENER The stonecutter didn't have anything good to say about the cook last night, he knows more than . . .

MASON You shouldn't be repeating what the stonecutter says, you can't trust an ex-con . . .

GARDENER That was a long time ago, and besides, the cook's a dragon always haggling over the price of vegetables . . .

OLD WOMAN Here comes the dyer from the police station . . . shush!

* * *

The STRANGER enters dressed in a redingote, top hat with mourning crepe, and a cane.

OLD WOMAN It's not the dyer, but he looks a lot like him.

* * *

STRANGER How much does a wreath like this one cost?

GARDENER Half a crown.

STRANGER It's not much.

GARDENER Well, you see I'm such an idiot I can't stick it to them.

STRANGER *(Looking around)* Has there been a — a fire here?

GARDENER Yes, it burnt down last night.

STRANGER My God.

> *Pause.*

Who owned the house?

GARDENER Valström, the factory owner.

STRANGER The dye-master?

GARDENER Yes, he's a dyer.

> *Pause.*

STRANGER Where is he?

GARDENER We expect him any minute.

STRANGER Then I'll go for a little walk, the wreath can stay there till I come back, I'm going out to the graveyard then.

GARDENER Out to the bishop's monument?

STRANGER What bishop?

GARDENER Bishop Stecksén. In the Academy, you know.

STRANGER Is he dead?

GARDENER Oh yes, for ages.

STRANGER I see. — Well, just leave the wreath there for now.

He goes out to the left, looking closely at the ruins.

* * *

OLD WOMAN Was he from the insurance maybe?

MASON Na-aw; he would have asked different things.

OLD WOMAN He did look a lot like the dyer, you know.

MASON But taller.

GARDENER I just remembered — I should have a wedding bouquet for this evening, for my son's wedding, but I don't have any flowers and my dark suit burned up. It's all . . . Mrs. Vesterlund is supposed to give us the myrtle for the crown, since she's the bride's godmother, and she stole the myrtle shoots from the dyer's cook who got it from the dyer's first wife, the one who ran off, and I was supposed to bind it up but I completely forgot — I'm the biggest idiot who's ever walked the earth —

He opens the door to the inn.

Mrs. Vesterlund, can I get that myrtle now and I'll fix it up. I said, can I get the myrtle! — Shouldn't there be a wreath too . . . Is there enough? — No? — Then the hell with this wedding, it doesn't matter anyway! — They can go to the priest and let him say a few words over them, but the stonecutter will go crazy. — What can I do about it? — I can't do that — haven't slept a wink all night. — It's too much for one man. — Yes, I'm an idiot, I already know that, go ahead and abuse me. — There's the pot, so, thanks a lot. Do you have any scissors? I don't have any with me, and some wire and string, where am I supposed to get them? — No one's running away from his job — I'm sick to death of the whole thing, when a man struggles for fifty years and then everything burns up; I can't begin to think about starting over; and when it comes all at once, blow by blow, I'm ready to just give it all up . . .

He goes.

* * *

The DYER enters, shaken, badly dressed, blue-black on his hands.

DYER Is it out now, Andersson?

MASON Now it's out.

DYER Has anything come to light?

MASON About? What you hide in the snow comes out with the thaw.

DYER What do you mean?

MASON The one who digs is the one who finds.

DYER Have you found something that clears up how the fire started?

MASON No, not as such.

DYER Then we're all still suspects, every one of us.

MASON Not me though?

DYER Yes, of course! You were seen wandering around at an unusual hour.

MASON I can't always go fetch the tools I've forgotten at a usual hour. When I fixed the heater in the student's room I forgot my hammer.

DYER And the stonecutter, and the gardener, and Madam Vesterlund, even the painter there, all are suspects, and the student and the cook and me most of all. Lucky thing I paid my insurance yesterday, or I'd be up a creek. — Just think, the stonecutter is suspected of arson and he's terrified of doing the slightest thing wrong; in fact he's so conscientious if you ask him what time it is, he'll answer but he won't swear to it since clocks can run slow. We all know about his two years inside, he got himself straightened out, and now I swear he's the most honorable man in the quarter.

MASON But the cops suspect him just because he once took a false step . . . and has a record.

DYER It's so strange, so strange to see things that way. — But you should go now, you have a wedding this evening.

MASON Yes, this wedding . . . There was someone here looking for you a minute ago, said he'd be right back.

DYER Who was it?

MASON He didn't say.

DYER From the police?

MASON Na-aw, I don't think so. — Oh, there he comes!

Goes off with the OLD WOMAN.

* * *

The STRANGER enters.

DYER *(Watching the STRANGER with curiosity, then with terror; he wants to run but can't)* Arvid!

STRANGER Rudolf!

DYER Is it really you?

STRANGER Yes.

Pause.

DYER So you're not dead?

STRANGER Yes, in some ways! — I've come from America after thirty years, something pulled me back, I needed to see my childhood home again ——— and now I find it in ruins.

Pause.

Burned during the night?

DYER Yes. You came just in time.

Pause.

STRANGER *(Slowly)* So that's the place — just imagine so little space for so many destinies! — There's the dining room with the painted walls, palm trees, cypresses, temples, under a rose-red sky; that's how I dreamed the world looked if I could just get away from home. — And the tile stove with the pale flowers growing out of seashells — the niche with the zinc doors — I remember when I was a child and we moved in, there was a name written in the zinc — and grandma said that a man with that name had killed himself in the room — I forgot it right away; but later in life when I married the daughter of the suicide's brother, I figured it was as if my own destiny had been written on that piece of metal — You don't believe in such things, well. — You do know at least how my marriage ended.

DYER Yes, I've heard . . .

STRANGER And there's the nursery. Yes.

DYER Let's not dig in the ruins.

STRANGER Why not? When there's been a fire you can read the ashes, that's what we used to do as children in the bonfires . . .

DYER Come sit at the table.

STRANGER What is this place? Ah yes, the Last Nail, where the hearse drivers stop by and in the old days convicts got a last drink before they were dragged off to the gallows . . . who owns it now?

DYER Madam Vesterlund, my old nurse.

STRANGER Madam Vesterlund. I remember her . . . It's as if the bench sinks beneath me and I'm falling down through time, sixty years, into childhood — I can feel the air in the nursery, the tightness in my chest — you older ones tormented me, and you made such awful noise, I was always terrified; I hid in the orchard; was dragged out and spanked, always spanked, but could never figure out why, I still don't know — still, she was my mother . . .

DYER Quiet!

STRANGER Yes, you were her favorite and were always praised . . . Then we got a stepmother. — Her father was a corpse hauler; and we'd seen him walking by on this road for many years . . . Eventually he became so well-known to us that he'd nod at us and grin as if to say "I'll be coming to take you too." And then one day he came into our house and we called him grandfather! Our father had married his daughter.

DYER It wasn't so remarkable.

STRANGER No, but how everything is woven together here, your own destiny and others' . . .

DYER It's like that everywhere.

STRANGER Absolutely, everywhere the same . . . When you're young you see the web being set up: parents, relatives, friends, acquaintances, servants are the warp; a little further on in life you see the woof; and the shuttle goes back and forth with the thread, it breaks sometimes but is knotted back together and on it goes; the beam strikes, the yarn is forced together into curlicues and there lies the web. In old age when the eyes begin to see, you discover that all the curlicues form a pattern, a monogram, an ornament, a hieroglyph, which now you can begin to understand: It's life itself! The Worldweaver has woven it!

Pause. The STRANGER rises.

Over there on the scrapheap I can see our family photograph album. *(Fetching the album)* Here is the book of our destiny! Grandfather and Grandmother, mother and father, siblings, relatives, acquaintances and so-called friends, schoolmates, maids, godparents . . . And what's remarkable is I've been in America, Australia, the Congo, Hong Kong, and wherever I've gone there's been a countryman, at least one, and when we got to talking, this countryman either knew one of my relatives or at least a godparent or a maid, an acquaintance in common, simply put. On the island of Formosa I met a relative . . .

DYER How have you come to these ideas?

STRANGER No matter how life's arranged itself — I've been rich and poor, up and down, suffered shipwrecks and earthquakes — and no matter how life's seemed to be I always found coherence and repetition. — In one situation I saw the consequences of an earlier one; when I met one person, I was reminded of another person from the past. There have even been scenes in my life that have returned several times, so that I've often said: I've been here before. And things have happened to me that have been inevitable or predetermined.

DYER What have you been doing all these years?

STRANGER Everything! I've seen life from all directions and points. From up above and down below, but always as if it were being staged especially for me; and through this I've finally been reconciled with parts of the past, and have come to excuse the so-called failings of others and of myself.— You and I for instance had considerable bouts ———

The DYER darkens and shrugs.

Now don't be afraid.

DYER I'm never afraid!

STRANGER So like yourself.

DYER And you too.

STRANGER Am I? That's interesting. — Yes, you live in your imagination where you're the bravest; and I remember when you first came up with this idea of diving into the swimming hole head first and mother said "Look at Rudolph, he's so brave!" That was directed at me, at me whom you'd deprived of courage and self-esteem. But then one day you stole some apples and were too cowardly to stand up to it so instead you blamed me.

DYER You haven't forgotten that?

STRANGER I haven't forgotten, but I have forgiven. — I can see the apple tree from here, that's why I remember it so well. It's right over there, a White Golden. — And if you look closely, you'll see where a big branch was sawed off. — I wasn't angry at you for the unjust punishment, but I was angry at the tree and cursed it. — Two years later, that great branch dried out and was cut away. I came to think of the fig tree our Savior cursed one time, but I drew no presumptuous conclusions. — In any case, I still know all the fruit trees by heart; when I was sick with yellow fever in Jamaica, I went through them one by one. Most of them are still here, I see. There's the Rosenhäger with its red-streaked fruit; where the spink made its nest; and over there I see the melon apple tree outside the attic window where I took my exams to be an engineer; there's the Hampus, and there's the Fall Astrakhan; the cinnamon pear tree that looks like a little pyramid poplar; and over there is the jam-pear that never got ripe and we all hated but mother valued most; there was a woodpecker in the old tree who'd crane her neck and screech something terrible . . . That was fifty years ago.

DYER *(Angrily)* What are you getting at?

STRANGER Just as suspicious and malicious as always. How interesting. — I have no purpose with my talk, memories tumble out . . . I remember once when the orchard was leased out; but we still had permission to take walks in it. It was like we'd been driven out of paradise — and the tempter hid behind every tree! In the fall when the apples lay ripe on the ground, I gave in to the temptation, it was unavoidable . . .

DYER So you stole too?

STRANGER Of course. But I didn't put the blame on you. — Some years later, about forty, when I owned a citrus plantation in the southern States, I had thieves in the orchards every night; I couldn't sleep, I grew thin, I got sick . . . Then I thought about Gustafsson, the poor gardener here.

DYER He's still alive!

STRANGER Maybe he stole apples in his childhood too?

DYER Undoubtedly.

STRANGER Why are your hands so black?

DYER Because I have to handle the dyes . . . Or do you mean something else?

STRANGER What would that be?

DYER That I don't have clean hands.

STRANGER Ah!

DYER You're thinking about the inheritance, perhaps.

STRANGER Just as petty! You're just like you were when you were eight.

DYER And you, just as carefree, just as philosophical, just as phony.

STRANGER It's so strange. — How many times have we said the same things we're saying now?

Pause.

I see here in this photo album . . . Siblings. Five are dead.

DYER Yes.

STRANGER And school friends?

DYER Some have been taken, some are still left.

STRANGER I met one in South Carolina. — Axel Eriksson. Remember him?

DYER Of course.

STRANGER He told me one long night during a train ride that our honored family, who enjoyed general esteem, were all a bunch of crooks, and that our fortune came from smuggling, and that this house was built with double walls to hide things in. Do you see? There are double walls.

DYER *(Crushed)* That's why there were so many closets everywhere.

STRANGER This Eriksson's father worked in the customs office and knew our father, and told the inside story that turned my whole imagined world upside down.

DYER Did you hit him at least?

STRANGER Why should I hit him? — In any case my hair turned grey that night as I re-edited my whole life. You know how we lived in mutual admiration and considered our family the best, and especially our ancestors whom we looked upon with an almost religious reverence. Now I had to repaint their faces, undress them, pull them down, and get them out of my mind. It was terrible! And then they began to haunt me; bits of those smashed idols reassembled themselves, but they didn't fit together. It was a wax museum of monstrosities. All those grey-haired men who came to our house and we called uncle, who played cards and ate supper, were smugglers, some had even worn neck-irons . . . Did you know that?

DYER *(Completely destroyed)* No.

STRANGER The whole dye business was only a cover for smuggling yarn, which was dyed so it wouldn't be recognized. — I remember I always hated the smell of the dye vats, something sickly sweet ———

DYER Why are you talking about all this now?

STRANGER Why should I keep quiet, and let you go around like an idiot bragging about your honored ancestors? Haven't you ever noticed how everyone smirks at you?

DYER No-o-o.

Pause.

STRANGER Over there in the scrapheap's our father's bookcase; you remember it was always locked. But one day, when father was away, I found the key. Those books that stood in the front I'd seen through the glass — Sermons and the works of great poets, and books about gardening, and collections about customs and confiscation, the Laws of the Land. A book on foreign coins. A book on technology, which later decided my career in life; but I discovered that behind these books there was a place for other things, and I investigated: first there was the cane switch — now I know that bitter plant bears a fruit that's used in the red dye called "dragon's blood," how strange! — Next to it was a bottle labeled "potassium cyanide."

DYER It was probably used in the dye works . . .

STRANGER And maybe for other things too. — But here's the point: there was a bundle of pamphlets with illustrated covers that peaked my interest ——— yes, without editorializing, it was the infamous memoirs of a certain cavalier — I took them out, closed the bookcase. And under the big oak over there I began my studies. It certainly was the Tree of Knowledge, *c'est vrai.*[1] And with that I left the paradise of childhood behind and was initiated, too early, into the secrets of . . . well.

DYER You too?

STRANGER So, you too!

> *Pause.*

Let's talk about something else, since everything is now reduced to ashes. — Were you insured?

DYER *(Angrily)* Didn't you ask that just a moment ago?

STRANGER I can't remember; I'm always confusing things I've said with things I've meant to say, especially since I think so intensely, ever since that day I hanged myself in the closet.

DYER What?

STRANGER I hanged myself in the closet.

DYER *(Slowly)* Is that what happened that Holy Thursday afternoon? And none of us kids found out? When you were taken to the hospital?

STRANGER *(Slowly)* Yes! — You see how little we know about our own family, our own home, our own life.

DYER Why did you do it?

STRANGER I was twelve years old, and suffered through life. It was like walking through a profound darkness . . . I didn't know what I should be doing with my life . . . and I thought the world was a madhouse! — I discovered this one day when the school was sent out with banners and flags to celebrate "our country's great warrior."[2] I'd just finished reading a book that described "our country's great warrior" as the worst king in our history — and here we were celebrating him with homages and hymns.

> *Pause.*

DYER What happened in the hospital?

STRANGER I lay in the morgue, dear brother, as if dead. Maybe I was, I don't know — but when I woke up I'd forgotten most of my previous life, and so I began a new one, but in such a way that you all thought I was strange. — Have you remarried?

DYER I have a wife and kids around here somewhere.

STRANGER When I regained consciousness, I thought I was another person: I took life with cynical calm; that's how things are, and the worse things got, the more interesting they were . . . I saw myself as someone else, and I observed this other person, studied him and his destiny, which made me insensitive to my own suffering. In death I had received new talents . . . I could see right through people, read their thoughts, hear their intentions . . . When I was in company, I saw them all naked . . . Where did the fire begin, anyway?

DYER No one knows.

STRANGER The paper said it started in the closet under the student's room in the attic, what student was that?

DYER Is it in the paper already? I haven't had time to look. What else does it say?

STRANGER Everything.

DYER Everything?

STRANGER The double walls, the honored family of smugglers, the neck-irons, the hairpins . . .

DYER What hairpins?

STRANGER I don't know, but that's what it says. Do you know?

DYER No.

STRANGER Everything into the light, and now they're expecting a stream of folks to gape at what the fire's exposed.

DYER Oh God. And I suppose you're happy that your family's the subject of scandal?

STRANGER My family? I've never felt related to you, never had feelings for my fellow beings or for myself, I only think it's interesting to watch them . . . What's your wife like?

DYER Was there something about her too?

STRANGER Her and the student.

DYER Beautiful! So I was right! You'll see! Just wait! — Here comes the stonecutter.

STRANGER You know him?

DYER And you do too. Our schoolmate, Albert Eriksson.

STRANGER Whose father worked for the customs office and whose brother I met on that train, the one who was so well informed about our family.

DYER So he's the devil that spilled it all to the newspapers.

* * *

The STONECUTTER enters with a mattock, examining the ruins.

STRANGER What a terrible look he has . . .

DYER He's done time, you know, two years . . . Do you know what he did? He falsified a contract I had with him . . .

STRANGER And you had him put in prison; now he has his revenge.

DYER What's strange is, now he's considered the most honorable man in the whole district; he's become a martyr and a saint almost and no one dares mess with him.

STRANGER Very interesting!

* * *

DETECTIVE *(Approaching the Stonecutter)* Are you thinking of tearing down this wall?

STONECUTTER The one by the closet?

DETECTIVE Yes.

STONECUTTER That's where the fire started, and I'm certain there's a candle or lamp in there; I know people, I do.

DETECTIVE Go ahead then.

STONECUTTER The closet burnt up, and the false floor collapsed, so we couldn't figure out what was what, but now we'll get at it.

He digs with the mattock.

Ah, there we go! — There we go. — Goodbye to that one. — Do you see anything?

DETECTIVE Not yet.

STONECUTTER *(As before)* Now do you see anything? — The lamp exploded, but the base is still there. — Who recognizes this pledge? — I thought the dye-master was over there.

DETECTIVE Yes, he's over there.

The DETECTIVE takes the base of the lamp and shows it to the DYER.

Do you recognize this lamp?

* * *

DYER It's not mine, it's the tutor's.

DETECTIVE The student's? Where is he?

DYER He's down in town, but he'll be back soon, his books are here.

DETECTIVE How did his lamp get in the cook's closet? Did he have a relationship with her?

DYER Probably.

DETECTIVE If he says the lamp's his, he'll be arrested. What do you think about all this?

DYER Me? What should I think?

DETECTIVE Well, what motive does he have for setting another man's house on fire?

DYER I don't know! Malice, a desire to harm, people are beyond reckoning . . . Maybe he wanted to hide something . . .

DETECTIVE It was a bad method, since all the old must come to light. — Did he bear you any kind of grudge?

DYER Likely. Since I'd helped him once when he was in need, and he hated me for it, of course.

DETECTIVE Of course! *(Pause)* Who was this student then?

DYER He was from the orphanage, born of unknown parents.

DETECTIVE Don't you have a grown daughter?

DYER *(Angrily)* Yes, of course I do.

DETECTIVE I see.

> Pause.

(To the STONECUTTER) Muster your strength and tear the walls down right away, so we can see what else comes to light.

> *The DETECTIVE exits.*

STONECUTTER It won't take but a minute.

> *The STONECUTTER exits.*

> Pause.

STRANGER Did you really pay the insurance?

DYER Of course.

STRANGER Yourself?

DYER No, I sent it as usual.

STRANGER You sent it — with someone else? That's so like you! — Shall we take a little stroll in the orchard and look at the apple trees?

DYER We can, and see what happens later.

STRANGER It's getting interesting now.

DYER Maybe not so interesting, if you're mixed up in it.

STRANGER Me?

DYER Who knows.

STRANGER What a web.

DYER You had a child in the orphanage, didn't you?

STRANGER My God! . . . Let's go for that walk in the orchard.

Curtain.

2.

The same scene, but with the walls torn down so that the spring flowers in the garden can be seen in bloom: daphne, deutzia, daffodils, narcissus, tulips, primroses, etc. and all the fruit trees are in bloom.

The STONECUTTER, MASON and OLD WOMAN, GARDENER, HEARSE DRIVER, MRS. VESTERLUND, and the PAINTER stand in a row looking at the empty plot of land.

STRANGER *(Enters)* There they stand, happy at the disaster, waiting for the sacrifice, which seems to be the main point. That it was arson they consider a fact, simply because they want it to be. — And all these crooks are my childhood friends, playmates; I'm related to the hearse driver through my stepmother, whose father hauled corpses ——— *(To those standing nearby)* Don't stand there, good people, there could be dynamite in the cellar, it could explode any moment.

The crowd disperses and disappears. The STRANGER stands by the scrapheap browsing through a book.

The student's books! — The same garbage we used when I was young — Livy's *History of Rome*, in which every single word is considered a lie. — This book is from my brother's collection — *Columbus, or the Discovery of America*! — But this is my book, I got it for Christmas in 1857; my name's scratched out; it was stolen from me and I accused the maid who was fired. Well, that's pretty, maybe her life was destroyed by it. Fifty years ago! — There's the frame of that old family portrait:

my famous grandfather, the smuggler who was once in neck-irons. Beautiful! — And what's this? Part of the frame of the mahogany bed — in which I was born. Damn! — Item: The foot of a dining room table — an ancestral heirloom — yes, it was always said to be ebony, wondered at because of it, and revealed now, after fifty years, by me, to be maple that's been dyed — everything was dyed in our house, so it wouldn't be recognized, even our baby clothes were dyed, so we always had dye on our skin! Ebony, humbug![3] — Here's the parlor clock, also smuggled goods, that measured out the hours of two generations; was wound every Saturday, when we had salted fish and beer soup for dinner — it seemed like an intelligent clock, it stopped when someone died; but when I died, it went right on — Let's have a look at you. What do you look like inside, old friend? *(The clock disintegrates as he touches it)* Can't stand up to inspection. Nothing can, nothing! Vanity, vanity! — There's the globe that sat up above, though it should have sat down below. You little earth! The densest of all the planets, the heaviest, and therefore so heavy upon you, too heavy to breathe, too heavy to bear; the cross is your symbol, but it could just as well have been a fool's cap or a straitjacket. — This world of illusions and madmen! — Eternal one! Has your earth gotten lost in space? And why does it spin around so, so your children get dizzy and lose their minds, and can never come to see what is, only what seems? Amen! There's the student.

* * *

The STUDENT enters looking for someone.

STRANGER He's looking for the wife! And tells everything he knows with his eyes. Happy youth! —Who are you looking for?

STUDENT *(Embarrassed)* I'm looking...

STRANGER Speak up, young man, or keep quiet! I understand equally well either way.

STUDENT With whom do I have the honor of speaking?

STRANGER It's no honor to speak to me, as you know, I ran off to America once upon a time because of unpaid debts...

STUDENT That was wrong...

STRANGER Right or wrong, it's a fact. You were looking for the lady of the house, she's not here, but she'll no doubt be coming back soon, like everyone else, they're drawn to fire like moths . . .

STUDENT — To the light!

STRANGER That's what *you* say, but I should rather have said to the lamp, to choose a more pregnant expression. — So, hide your feelings if you can, young man, I can hide mine! — We were talking about the lamp, weren't we? What about the lamp?

STUDENT What lamp?

STRANGER That's right. Deny and lie about everything. — The lamp you put in the cook's closet when you set fire to the house.

STUDENT I don't know anything about that.

STRANGER Some blush when they lie, others turn pale — But this one has found something altogether new.

STUDENT Are you talking to yourself, sir?

STRANGER It's a bad habit of mine. — If I may ask, are your parents still alive?

STUDENT No, I'm afraid they're not.

STRANGER Another lie, though he doesn't know it.

STUDENT I never lie!

STRANGER Only three times in barely a minute. I know your father.

STUDENT I doubt it.

STRANGER All the better for me. — Do you see this stick pin? Beautiful, isn't it. But I never get to see it myself, never can enjoy seeing it though everyone else gets to. At least it's not egotistical, but there are times I'd like to see it on someone else so I can admire it. Would you like it?

STUDENT I don't understand . . . Maybe it's better not to have it, as you say.

STRANGER Perhaps so. — Don't be impatient, she'll be here soon. —

Is it enviable to be young?

STUDENT No, not that I've found.

STRANGER Not in charge of your own life, having to eat the bread of others, never having any money, never able to speak your mind, always treated like a naïve fool, and since you can't get married, you must look to others' wives with all the danger that entails. Youth, humbug!

STUDENT That's the truth. When you're a child, you wish you were grownup, like maybe fifteen, and could go away to study, own a grownup hat; then later you wish you were old, like maybe twenty-one. No one wants to be young.

STRANGER And when you really are old, you wish you were dead. There's not much left to want then? — Do you know you're going to be arrested?

STUDENT Am I?

STRANGER Yes, the police said so just now.

STUDENT Me?

STRANGER Are you surprised? Don't you know that here in life you have to be ready for anything?

STUDENT What have I done?

STRANGER You don't have to have done something to be arrested; you only have to be suspected.

STUDENT Then everyone could be arrested.

STRANGER Absolutely right. One should put a rope around the neck of the whole breed, if one really wanted to be just, but no one does. It's a horrible breed anyway, ugly, sweaty, stinking; dirty linen, filthy stockings with holes in them, corns, bunions, Usch! No, an apple tree in bloom is much more beautiful; look at the lilies out in the field, it's as if they weren't at home here, and how sweetly they smell.

STUDENT Are you a philosopher?

STRANGER A great philosopher.

STUDENT Now you're making fun of me.

STRANGER You said that just so you could get away. Go on then. Hurry off.

STUDENT I was waiting for someone here.

STRANGER Yes, just as I thought. — But it's probably best you go and meet her half way.

STUDENT Did she ask you to tell me that?

STRANGER No need.

STUDENT I'm not going to mess this up . . . if it's so . . .

* * *

STRANGER Is he my child? In the worst case I was once a child myself, and it was neither remarkable nor particularly fun. — So I am his . . . ! What more? Besides . . . who knows? ——— Now I'll just say hello to Madam Vesterlund — she was a servant in my parent's house, trustworthy and of good character, and after she'd stolen from us for ten years she was named the faithful servant.

He sits at one of the tables.

Here's Gustafsson's wreaths — bearberry though he says they're lingonberry — just as sloppy as forty years ago — everything he did was sloppy or stupid, and so things went badly for him. But his self-knowledge forgives much: I'm such a cow, he used to say, and then he'd take off his cap and scratch his head. — Here's a myrtle plant. *(He taps the pot)* Unwatered, of course — he always forgot to water things, the cow . . . and still he thought they should grow!

The PAINTER enters.

Who's the painter? Also from the Morass, perhaps another thread in my web. —

The PAINTER stares at the STRANGER, who stares back.

Do you recognize me?

PAINTER Is that you — Mr. Arvid?

STRANGER It is, if to be is to be perceived.

Pause.

PAINTER I really ought to be angry with you.

STRANGER Suit yourself. But do tell me why. Often that straightens things out.

PAINTER Do you remember ———

STRANGER Unfortunately I have an exceptional memory.

PAINTER Do you remember a boy named Robert?

STRANGER Of course, a big lunk who could draw well.

PAINTER *(Slowly)* And who was going to go to the Academy to be a painter, an artist. But back then color-blindness was all the rage. Since you were a technolog, Mr. Arvid, you had to examine my eyes before my patron, your father, would allow me to go to art school... You took two balls of yarn from the dye works; a red one and a green one, and then you quizzed me and I called the green one red and vice versa. With that my career was destroyed...

STRANGER And so it should have been.

PAINTER No — for the fact is, I could tell the difference between the colors, I just couldn't distinguish between the *names*.[4] This was only discovered when I was thirty...

STRANGER It's a sad story, but I didn't know any better, so you should forgive me.

PAINTER How can I?

STRANGER Misjudgments can be forgiven. — Listen to me now. I wanted to join the navy: test-sailed as a cadet; got a bit seasick and was discharged. But I had no trouble at sea; the seasickness was from having drunk too much. With that my career was destroyed and I chose another...

PAINTER What's the navy got to do with me? I dreamed about Rome and Paris...

STRANGER Well, people dream a lot of things when they're young, and when they're old too. Besides, it was a long time ago, why bring it up now.

PAINTER Imagine saying such a thing. Maybe you can give me back a lost life...

STRANGER That I can't. But I don't owe you anything. I learned the thing with the yarn in school. Anyway, you should have been able to name your colors. — So there's the road, now take a hike as far as the road is long — one less paint-smearer in the world can only be a godsend for humankind! — There's Madam Vesterlund.

PAINTER Yes you can talk, but you'll get yours.

* * *

MRS. VESTERLUND enters.

STRANGER Hello, Madam Vesterlund; it's me, Arvid, don't be afraid; I've been in America, how are things; wonderful with me, there's been a fire here, and your husband has died, he was in the police department, a decent man, I liked him, he had a good-natured, friendly way about him, he was a harmless joker who never hurt anyone, I remember one time...

MRS. VESTERLUND Dear God! Is it really you, Arvid, who I took care of...

STRANGER No, that wasn't me, that was my brother, but it doesn't matter, just as dear, I was talking about your old man who died, thirty-years ago, he was a fine man, a good friend...

MRS. VESTERLUND Yes, he died. *(Pause)* but I'm not so sure. — Maybe you're confusing him...

STRANGER No, I'm not confusing him... I remember old man Vesterlund well, and I liked him a lot...

MRS. VESTERLUND *(Slowly)* It's a shame to say so, but he really wasn't all that good-natured.

STRANGER Him?

MRS. VESTERLUND Yes . . . he had a way of getting in good with people, but he never meant what he said . . . or he said the opposite . . .

STRANGER What? Didn't mean what he said? He was dishonest?

MRS. VESTERLUND A shame to say, but it seems to me . . .

STRANGER You mean he wasn't honest?

MRS. VESTERLUND No-o-o. He — was — a little — well, he didn't always mean what he said. But you, Mr. Arvid, how have you been?

STRANGER A light's gone off in my head! — The lying cheat. And I've gone around for thirty-five years speaking well of him, missing him, I mourned at his funeral, bought a wreath for his casket with my tobacco money . . .

MRS. VESTERLUND What? What was it?

STRANGER What a crook! *(Pause)* Well, he fooled me one Mardi Gras, said if you take away every third egg from the hens they'll lay more. I did it and got a beating, and almost went to jail . . . But I never suspected he was the informant . . . he hung out in the kitchen hoping for a handout — the maids could do whatever they wanted with the leftovers — now I see his true colors. — And here I am angry at someone who's been in the grave for thirty-five years! — He was so satirical, I didn't understand it then but I understand it now.

MRS. VESTERLUND Yes, he was always a bit satirical, I knew that.

STRANGER Now I'm remembering more . . . And here I've been talking well about this idiot for thirty-five years. And I went to his funeral, had my first drink . . . And I remember, he used to flatter me, called me professor, the heir-apparent . . . Usch! ——— Here comes the stonecutter. Go in now, Madam, or there'll be a fight when he gets here with his reckonings. Go, Madam, we'll meet again.

MRS. VESTERLUND *(Going in)* No, we shall not meet again, one should never meet again — it's not the same as before, and they only tear things down for you; why did you have to go and say all that, when things were so clear before . . .

She goes.

* * *

The STONECUTTER enters.

STRANGER Over here.

STONECUTTER What is it?

STRANGER Come on.

The STONECUTTER stares at him.

Are you looking at my stick pin? — I bought it in London at Charing Cross . . .

STONECUTTER I'm no thief.

STRANGER No but you've mastered the noble art of falsification . . . you scratch things out.

STONECUTTER That's true, but it was a thief's contract that was strangling me . . .

STRANGER Why did you sign it?

STONECUTTER I was desperate.

STRANGER That's one motive.

STONECUTTER But now I've got my revenge.

STRANGER How pretty.

STONECUTTER And now they're in for it.

STRANGER Did we ever fight as children?

STONECUTTER No, I was too young.

STRANGER Have we never lied to each other, or stolen something, or crushed each other's careers, or seduced each other's sisters?

STONECUTTER No, but my father worked for the customs office and your father was a smuggler . . .

STRANGER See, always something.

STONECUTTER And when my father couldn't make an arrest, he was fired.

STRANGER Are you looking for revenge on me, because your father was a fool.

STONECUTTER Why did you say there was dynamite in the cellar?

STRANGER Another lie! I said there *could* be, after all anything is possible.

STONECUTTER You know, the student's been arrested. Did you know him?

STRANGER Very little, but his mother was a maid in our house. She was beautiful and kind, I proposed to her once; in time she had a child.

STONECUTTER Then you're not the father?

STRANGER No-o-o. But since paternity can never be denied, I'm like a stepfather.

STONECUTTER So people have lied about you?

STRANGER Of course. But it's a common fault . . .

STONECUTTER And I testified against you . . . under oath.

STRANGER I can imagine; but what does it matter? Nothing really matters. — Now let's stop tearing up the old tracks — it'll just add fuel to the fire.

STONECUTTER But I committed perjury . . .

STRANGER Yes, it's not pleasant, but such things happen . . .

STONECUTTER It's terrible! Isn't it terrible to be alive?

STRANGER (*With his hand over his eyes*) Yes! Beyond all description, terrible.

STONECUTTER I don't want to live any longer . . .

STRANGER You must! *(Pause)* You must!

Pause.

Listen, the student's been arrested, can he be released?

STONECUTTER With difficulty. — I'm going to say something because we're talking so openly: he isn't guilty, but he can't free himself; the only witness who could prove his innocence would thereby prove her own guilt — of something else.

STRANGER The one with the hairpins?

STONECUTTER Yes.

STRANGER Old or young?

STONECUTTER You'll have to figure that out yourself, but it's not the cook.

STRANGER What a tangled web! — But who put the lamp there?

STONECUTTER His worst enemy.

STRANGER Did his worst enemy start the fire?

STONECUTTER See, that I don't know. — Only the mason knows.

STRANGER Who is the mason?

STONECUTTER He's the oldest in the quarter, related somehow to Madam Vesterlund, knows the secrets of the whole house; has some kind of secret himself with the dye-master, so he won't be a witness.

STRANGER And who is the woman, my sister-in-law?

STONECUTTER Yes, well — she was nanny in the house before the first wife took off.

STRANGER What's she like?

STONECUTTER Hmm! Like? Yes, well, I don't really know. Do you mean profession? Name and profession are recorded on the census forms, but that's not what you're like, it's what you do.

STRANGER I mean temperament.

STONECUTTER I see, well, temperament changes; with me it depends on who I'm talking to. With a decent fellow I'm decent, but with a nasty one I'm a beast.

STRANGER We were talking about the woman's temperament, in general.

STONECUTTER Yes, well, anyway: like most people; she gets mad if you provoke her; then she's fine again; you can't always be in the same mood.

STRANGER I mean is she lighthearted or melancholy?

STONECUTTER When things go well for her, she's happy, and when things don't, she's sad or angry like all of us.

STRANGER Yes, but how is she generally?

STONECUTTER Well I suppose it comes down to the same thing. — As an educated person, she behaves well, though she can be coarse, even her, when her temper flares.

STRANGER I don't get it.

STONECUTTER *(Slapping him on the back)* No sir, one doesn't get it when it comes to other people.

STRANGER He's superb! — So, what do you think about the dye-master, my brother?

    Pause.

STONECUTTER Well, he has good manners. Beyond that, I don't know; whatever he's hiding, I can't figure it out

STRANGER Excellent! — He always has blue hands, but you know they're white underneath.

STONECUTTER Then they should be scraped first, but he won't allow that.

STRANGER Good! — Who are those young people over there?

STONECUTTER That's the gardener's son and my daughter; they were supposed to get married this evening, but had to postpone because of the fire. — I'm going to go so I don't embarrass them. — You understand, a father-in-law like me. — Goodbye.

> *He goes. The STRANGER withdraws behind the inn but remains visible to the audience. ALFRED and MATILDA enter, holding hands.*

ALFRED I had to come see where the fire was — I had to —

MATILDA What's there to see?

ALFRED I've had it so hard in this house that many times I wished it would burn down . . .

MATILDA It shaded the garden. Now it'll grow better, as long as they don't build a bigger house . . .

ALFRED It's beautiful and free here, airy and sunny; I've heard they're going to put a street through . . .

MATILDA Then you're going to have to move?

ALFRED We're all going to move, and I'm glad, I like the new, I'd like to emigrate . . .

MATILDA Oh no! You know our doves nested on the roof there, and when it burned last night, they flew all around, but when the roof fell in, they flew right into the fire. ——— They couldn't stand being separated from their old home!

ALFRED We have to get away from here — away! Father says the earth here is tapped out . . .

MATILDA I've heard that the stubble after a fire should be taken out to the fields to improve the soil . . .

ALFRED You mean the ashes . . .

MATILDA Yes, it's supposed to be good to sow in the ashes...

ALFRED New earth is better ———

MATILDA But your father is ruined...

ALFRED Not at all, he has money in the bank. — Of course he complains, everyone does.

MATILDA He has... So he wasn't ruined by the fire?

ALFRED Not a bit! But he's a sly old dog, though he calls himself a cow...

MATILDA I don't know what to think.

ALFRED He's even lent money to the mason... and to others too.

MATILDA I don't know where I am... am I dreaming? — We cried all morning over your father's bad fortune, and over our postponed wedding...

ALFRED My poor darling. Our wedding's this evening...

MATILDA You mean it's not been postponed?

ALFRED It's postponed two hours so my father has time to find a new coat...

MATILDA Oh and how we cried...

ALFRED Unnecessary tears. So many tears.

MATILDA It's troubling that they were unnecessary, despite... imagine your father being such a rogue...

ALFRED Yes, he's quite a joker, to say the least. — He's always saying he's tired, but he's just lazy, so lazy...

MATILDA Don't say anything else bad about your father — let's get out of here. — I have to change clothes and put up my hair. — Imagine your father not being who I thought — going around pretending and fooling like that! — Maybe you're like that too — and people don't know who you are.

ALFRED You'll find that out later!

MATILDA But then it'll be too late!

ALFRED Never too late . . .

MATILDA You're so nasty when you're here . . . I'm afraid of you . . .

ALFRED Not of me . . .

MATILDA I don't know what to think . . . Why haven't you said anything about your father being well off before . . .

ALFRED I wanted to test you, to see if you liked me even though I was poor.

MATILDA Afterwards you say it was a test; but I'm not sure I can ever trust anyone again . . .

ALFRED Go and change your clothes. I'll order the carriage.

MATILDA Are we going by carriage?

ALFRED Of course! Closed carriage!

MATILDA Closed carriage? And this evening? How wonderful! Hurry back! A closed carriage!

ALFRED *(Taking her by the hand, they skip out)* I'm back already!

* * *

STRANGER Bravo!

* * *

The DETECTIVE enters and speaks quietly with the STRANGER, who responds just as quietly. This goes on for about half a minute then the DETECTIVE exits. The WIFE enters, dressed in black. She stares at the STRANGER.

WIFE Are you my brother-in-law?

STRANGER Yes I am. *(Pause)* Don't I match the descriptions, or depictions?

WIFE Truthfully: no.

STRANGER One usually doesn't; and I have to confess the description of you I received a bit ago isn't much like the original either.

WIFE Yes, people do one another such wrong, painting each other over, always in their own likeness . . .

STRANGER And they act like theater directors handing out roles; some accept their roles, others hand them back preferring to improvise ———

WIFE What kind of roles have you played?

STRANGER The seducer! — Not because I was one; I've never seduced anyone, neither girl nor wife, but once when I was young I was seduced, and so I got the role. Fact is, it was forced on me, so I took it; and for twenty years I've lived with the guilty conscience of a seducer . . .

WIFE You were innocent?

STRANGER Yes.

WIFE How strange. To this day my husband talks about how Nemesis pursues you because you seduced another man's wife.

STRANGER I can believe it. — But your husband is a particularly interesting case: He's cobbled a character for himself out of lies; isn't it true he's a coward in all life's battles?

WIFE Yes, a coward.

STRANGER And brags about his courage, which is only brutality.

WIFE You know him well.

STRANGER Yes and no. — And you've lived believing you've married into a revered family that has always behaved honorably.

WIFE I had thought so until this morning — .

STRANGER Then it all came tumbling down! — What a web of lies, mistakes, misunderstandings. And we're supposed to take it seriously.

WIFE Do you?

STRANGER Sometimes. Seldom these days . . . I'm like a sleepwalker on the edge of a roof — I know I'm sleeping, but I'm not — and I am only waiting to be awakened.

WIFE You're said to have been on the other side . . .

STRANGER I've been across the river, but I don't remember anything other than — that there everything was what it's said to be. That's the difference.

WIFE When nothing can stand up to being inspected, what are people supposed to hold on to?

STRANGER Don't you know?

WIFE Tell me. Tell me.

STRANGER Suffering leads to patience; patience provides experience; experience leads to hope; and hope doesn't allow itself to be shamed.

WIFE Hope, yes.

STRANGER Yes, hope.

WIFE Aren't you ever happy to be alive?

STRANGER Of course, but even that's an illusion. I'll tell you, dear sister-in-law, when you're born without a membrane over your eyes, you see life and people for what they are . . . you'd have to be a pig to enjoy this filth. — When you've had enough of the smoke and mirrors,[5] you turn your eyes outside in and look into your own soul. Now there's something to see . . .

WIFE What do you see there?

STRANGER Yourself! But once you've seen yourself, you die.

The WIFE holds her hands in front of her eyes. Pause.

WIFE Will you help me?

STRANGER If I can.

WIFE Try.

STRANGER Wait then — No, I can't. — He's been arrested but he's innocent; only you could free him, but you can't. It's a net not tied by human hands . . .

WIFE But he's not guilty ...

STRANGER Who is not guilty?

WIFE No one! ——— It was an accident, the fire.

STRANGER I know —

WIFE What should we do?

STRANGER Suffer. It will pass. Even this is vanity.

WIFE Suffer?

STRANGER Suffer. But hope.

WIFE *(Stretching out her hand)* Thank you.

STRANGER And to console you —

WIFE What?

STRANGER No one suffers without guilt.

> *The WIFE bows her head and exits.*

* * *

> *The STRANGER goes over to the ruins.*

* * *

DYER *(Enters, happy)* Are you haunting the ruins now?

STRANGER Ghosts thrive in ruins. — You seem happy.

DYER I am.

STRANGER And brave?

DYER Who should I fear, or what?

STRANGER Your happiness suggests you're ignorant of one important detail. — Are you brave enough to bear a set-back?

DYER What's this about?

STRANGER You're not turning pale?

DYER Me?

STRANGER A big set-back?

DYER Tell me.

STRANGER That detective was here just now, and informed me . . . just between the two of us . . .

DYER What?

STRANGER Your insurance payment was filed two hours too late . . .

DYER Christ . . . what are you saying? — I sent my wife with the money.

STRANGER And she sent the bookkeeper . . . and he arrived too late.

DYER Then I'm ruined.

Pause.

STRANGER Are you crying?

DYER I'm ruined.

STRANGER Yes. Can't you bear it?

DYER What am I going to live on? What am I going to do?

STRANGER Work.

DYER I'm too old; I have no friends . . .

STRANGER Maybe you'll find some now. An unhappy man is always sympathetic; I've had my best moments when I was unhappy.

DYER *(Wild)* I'm ruined!

STRANGER But in good company and happy times, I was always alone; envy couldn't hide itself behind friendship . . .

DYER I'll have the bookkeeper arrested

STRANGER Don't do that.

DYER He'll pay . . .

STRANGER So like yourself. What's the point of having lived when you haven't learned a thing.

DYER I'll have him arrested, he's a lying cheat, he's always hated me just because I boxed him on the ears once . . .

STRANGER Forgive him — as I have you, when I resigned my inheritance.

DYER What inheritance?

STRANGER Irredeemable! Merciless! Cowardly! Mendacious! — Go in peace, brother.

DYER What's this inheritance you're talking about?

STRANGER Listen now, Rudolf, brother, my mother's son in any case, you put the stonecutter in jail because he falsified a document . . . well . . . you falsified my copy of *Christopher Columbus, or the Discovery of America*.

DYER *(Struck)* Wha—what? Columbus?

STRANGER Yes, my book, that became yours.

    The DYER says nothing.

Putting the student's lamp in the closet I can understand, I can understand everything, but did you know that the dining room table wasn't made of ebony?

DYER Wasn't it?

STRANGER Maple.

DYER Maple?

STRANGER The most treasured possession in the house, valued at 2,000 crowns.

DYER That too? More humbug.

STRANGER Yes.

DYER Usch!

STRANGER The debt is paid. The case is closed, the thing can't be unraveled, the parties withdraw . . .

DYER *(Rushing out)* I'm ruined!

STRANGER *(Taking his wreath from the table)* I thought I'd go out to the graveyard with this wreath, to the parents' grave; but I think I'll just lay it here on the ruins of my ancestral home, my childhood home.

(A silent bow) And so: back out into the world, wanderer.

The Ghost Sonata

Opus 3 of the Chamber Plays (1907)

The Ghost Sonata

Characters

Director Hummel, THE OLD MAN.
THE STUDENT, Arkenholz.
THE MILKMAID.
THE CONCIERGE.
THE PORTER.[1]
THE DEAD MAN, Consul.
THE LADY IN BLACK, daughter of the Dead Man with the Concierge.
THE COLONEL.
THE MUMMY, the Colonel's wife.
HIS DAUGHTER, really the Old Man's daughter.
THE NOBLEMAN, called Baron Skanskorg, engaged to the Concierge's daughter.
JOHANSSON, servant to Hummel.
BENGTSSON, employed at the Colonel's house.
THE FIANCÉE, Hummel's former fiancée, a white-haired old woman.
THE COOK.

1.

The ground floor and first story façade of a modern apartment building, though only the corner of the building is seen. It ends in a round room on the ground floor with a balcony and flag pole above.

When the shades are up, a white marble statue of a young woman is visible through the open window into the Round Room. It is surrounded by palms and brightly lit by sunlight. In the window to the left are pots of hyacinths (blue, white, pink).

In the corner one flight up on the railing of the balcony are a blue silk bedcover and two white pillows. The window to the left is hung with white sheets.

It is a clear Sunday morning.

In front of the façade in the foreground is a green bench. To the right in the foreground is a public water fountain; to the left is an advertising column.[2]

In the background to the left is an entryway that reveals a white marble stairway with a brass and mahogany banister. On the pavement on either side of the door are laurel bushes in decorative pots.

The corner with the Round Room faces onto a cross street that seems to go off into the background.

On the bottom floor to the left of the entryway is a window with a gossip-mirror.[3]

As the curtain rises, the bells of several distant churches can be heard.

The doors to the façade are open. The LADY IN BLACK stands nervously on the stairs.

The CONCIERGE sweeps the foyer then polishes the brass fittings on the door and waters the laurel bushes.

The OLD MAN sits in a wheel chair by the advertising kiosk reading a newspaper; he has white hair and beard and eyeglasses.

The MILKMAID enters around the corner with bottles in a wire basket; she is in summer clothes with brown shoes, black stockings and white beret. The milkmaid takes off the beret and hangs it on the fountain; she wipes the sweat from her brow, drinks a cup of water, washes her hands, and straightens her hair using the water as a mirror.

A steamboat bell is heard, and now and then the bass notes from an organ in a nearby church penetrate the silence.

After a few minutes of silence, when the MILKMAID has finished washing, the STUDENT enters from the left, unshaven and uncombed. He goes to the fountain.

Pause.

STUDENT May I use the cup?

The MILKMAID pulls the cup to herself.

Aren't you finished with it?

The MILKMAID looks at him in terror.

OLD MAN *(To himself)* Who is he talking to? — I don't see anyone! Is he crazy?

The OLD MAN continues to watch them in wonder.

STUDENT What are you looking at? Do I look that bad? — I know, I didn't sleep last night. You probably think I've been out carousing...

The MILKMAID, as before.

Drinking, huh? Do I smell like alcohol?

The MILKMAID, as before.

I didn't shave, I know . . . Give me a drink of water, girl, I've earned it! *(Pause)* Well then, I guess I'll have to tell you. I spent all night binding wounds and tending to the dying; I was there when the building collapsed last night . . . now you know.

The MILKMAID rinses the cup and gives him a drink.

Thanks!

The MILKMAID is uneasy.

(Slowly) Could you do me a big favor? *(Pause)* My eyes are inflamed, as you can see, but my hands — they're smeared with death, I can't clear my eyes with them . . . Will you moisten my handkerchief and bathe my feverish eyes? Will you be the Good Samaritan?

The MILKMAID hesitates but does as he asked.

Thank you, my friend!

He takes out his wallet. The MILKMAID makes a gesture of refusal.

Forgive me. That was ungrateful. I'm exhausted . . .

The MILKMAID exits.

*

OLD MAN *(To the STUDENT)* Excuse my intrusion, but I couldn't help but overhear. You were at the accident last night . . . I was just reading about it in the paper . . .

STUDENT Is it there already?

OLD MAN Yes, the whole story; and a picture of you, but they regret they weren't able to find out the name of the heroic young man . . .

STUDENT *(Looking at the paper)* Yes, it's me! Well!

OLD MAN Who were you speaking to just now?

STUDENT Didn't you see?

Pause.

OLD MAN I trust you won't think it impertinent of me to ask — to enquire — your name?

STUDENT Why? I don't like publicity — gain renown and criticism follows — slander is a highly developed art form these days — besides, I don't want a reward . . .

OLD MAN You're wealthy then?

STUDENT Not at all . . . In fact . . . I'm broke.

OLD MAN In that case . . . You know I think I've heard that voice before . . . I had a friend when I was a child who couldn't say the word "window," he'd always say "windoor" — I've only run into one person with that peculiarity. You remind me of him — is it possible you're related to the grocer Arkenholz.

STUDENT He was my father.

OLD MAN Strange are the ways of fate . . . I saw you as a tiny infant, under particularly difficult circumstances.

STUDENT It's said I came into the world during bankruptcy proceedings.

OLD MAN Precisely!

STUDENT Perhaps I could ask your name?

OLD MAN Director Hummel . . .

STUDENT Really . . . ? Yes, now I remember . . .

OLD MAN You've heard my name spoken often in your family?

STUDENT Yes!

OLD MAN And perhaps spoken with a certain disdain?

>   *The STUDENT keeps silent.*

Yes, I can imagine — They say I was the one who ruined your father? — Anyone who ruins himself with stupid investments always thinks he's been ruined by the one person he couldn't con. *(Pause)* The fact is, your father took me for 17,000 crowns, my life savings at the time.

STUDENT It's amazing how the same story can be told in two such opposite ways.

OLD MAN Certainly you don't believe I'm not telling the truth?

STUDENT What should I believe? My father didn't lie!

OLD MAN That's true, a father never lies . . . but I am also a father, therefore . . .

STUDENT What are you getting at?

OLD MAN I saved your father from misery, and he paid me back with the terrible hatred of guilty gratitude . . . he taught his family to speak ill of me.

STUDENT Perhaps you made him ungrateful by poisoning the help you gave with unnecessary humiliations.

OLD MAN All help is humiliating, young man.

STUDENT What do you want from me?

OLD MAN I don't need money; but if you would do me some small services, I'll consider myself well repaid. You see me as a cripple, some say it's my own fault, others blame my parents. Personally, I believe it is life itself waiting in ambush. If you manage to avoid one trap, you fall right into another. In any case, I can't run up stairs, can't ring door bells, so I'm asking you for help!

STUDENT What do I have to do?

OLD MAN First, push me over there so I can read the posters; I want to see what's playing this afternoon . . .

STUDENT *(Pushing the wheel chair)* Don't you have a man to do this?

OLD MAN Yes, but he's off running an errand . . . coming right back . . . are you a medical student?

STUDENT No I'm studying languages, but I have no idea what I'll do afterwards . . .

OLD MAN *(Laughing)* How's your math?

STUDENT Tolerable.

OLD MAN Fine! — Would you, perhaps, be interested in a job?

STUDENT Sure, why not?

OLD MAN Fine. *(Reading the posters)* There's a matinee of *The Valkyrie*[4] today . . . The Colonel and his daughter will be there, and since he always sits on the aisle in the sixth row, I'll put you next to them . . . Why don't you go into the telephone booth and order a ticket in the sixth row, seat number 82.

STUDENT You want me to go to the opera this afternoon?

OLD MAN Yes! If you trust me, all will go well! I want you to be happy, wealthy and wise: your debut yesterday as the brave knight makes you famous today and your name is worth a lot.

STUDENT *(Goes to the telephone kiosk)* This could turn out to be an amusing adventure . . .

OLD MAN Are you the sporting type?

STUDENT Yes, it was my undoing.

OLD MAN So your luck will change! — Now call.

> *The OLD MAN reads the newspaper. The LADY IN BLACK has come out onto the steps and talks to the CONCIERGE. The OLD MAN listens, but the audience hears nothing. The STUDENT returns.*

All set?

STUDENT Done.

OLD MAN Do you see that house?

STUDENT Of course I've noticed it . . . I went by here yesterday, when the sun glistened on the windows — and imagined all the beauty and opulence in there — I said to my friend: It must be something to own an apartment there, third floor, with a beautiful young wife, two lovely children, and an investment income of 20,000 crowns a year . . .

OLD MAN Did you say that? Did you? Well! I love this house too . . .

STUDENT Do you speculate in houses?

OLD MAN Yes and no. Not in the way you think . . .

STUDENT Do you know the people who live here?

OLD MAN All of them. At my age, one knows everyone, their fathers and their grandfathers, and you're always related to them in some way — I'm now eighty years old — but no one really knows me, not really — I take an interest in people's fate . . .

> *The shades in the Round Room are drawn up: The COLONEL appears in civilian clothes; after looking at the thermometer, he goes into the room and stands in front of the marble statue.*

Look, there's the Colonel you'll sit next to this afternoon . . .

STUDENT Is that him — the Colonel? I don't understand any of this. It's like a fairy tale . . .

OLD MAN My whole life is like a book of fairy tales, young man; and though the stories are all different, there's a thread running through them and the main motif returns like clockwork.

STUDENT Who's the statue of in there?

OLD MAN His wife, naturally . . .

STUDENT Was she so beautiful, then?

OLD MAN Oh yes!

STUDENT Really?

OLD MAN We can't judge another, dear boy. — If I were to tell you that she left, that he beat her, that she returned, married him again, and that now she sits in there like a mummy worshipping her own statue, you'd think I was crazy.

STUDENT I don't understand!

OLD MAN I'm not surprised. — And there we have the hyacinth window. His daughter lives there . . . she's out riding at the moment but she'll be home soon.

STUDENT Who was that woman in black talking with the concierge?

OLD MAN Yes, well that's a little complicated, but it's connected to the recently deceased, up there where the sheets are . . .

STUDENT Who was he, then?

OLD MAN A human being, like us, but what showed most was his vanity . . . If you were a Sunday child, you would soon see him come out to look at the flag flying at half mast on the consulate — he was the consul, after all, and liked such formalities — crowns and lions, plumed hats, and colored arm bands.

STUDENT You said something about a Sunday child — I'm told I was born on a Sunday . . .

OLD MAN No! Are you . . . ? I should have known . . . I saw it in the color of your eyes . . . but then you can see what others can't, haven't you noticed that?

STUDENT I don't know what others see, but sometimes . . . well, one doesn't usually talk about such things!

OLD MAN I was almost certain of it! But you can tell me . . . I — understand such things . . .

STUDENT Yesterday for example . . . I was drawn to that unremarkable street where the building collapsed . . . stood in front of a building I'd never seen before . . . Then I noticed a crack in the wall, heard the foundations split; I ran up and grabbed a child who was walking next to the wall . . . A second later the whole building fell . . . I was saved, but in my arms, where I thought I had the child, there was nothing . . .

OLD MAN If I may say so . . . I thought as much . . . Explain something to me: what were you gesturing at just now by the fountain? And why were you talking to yourself?

STUDENT Didn't you see the milkmaid?

OLD MAN *(Terrified)* Milkmaid?

STUDENT Of course, the one who gave me the cup of water.

OLD MAN So that's how it is? . . . Well then, maybe I can't see but there are other things I can do . . .

> *The WHITE-HAIRED WOMAN appears at the window with the gossip'-mirror and sits down.*

Look at that old woman in the window! Do you see her? — She was my fiancée, once, sixty years ago . . . I was twenty. — Don't worry, she doesn't recognize me! We see each other every day, but without the least effect on me, even though we once pledged everlasting troth to one another — everlasting!

STUDENT Your generation was so unreasonable in the old days! We don't talk about such things now with our girls.

OLD MAN Forgive us, youngster, we didn't know any better! — But can you see that that old woman was once young and beautiful?

STUDENT It doesn't show. Well yes, there is something beautiful about her, but I can't see her eyes!

The CONCIERGE comes out with a basket and spreads spruce branches.[5]

OLD MAN The concierge, yes! — The woman in black there is her daughter by the dead man. That's why her husband got the job as caretaker . . . but the lady in black has a lover who's nobility and waiting to get rich. He's in the process of divorcing his wife, who's throwing him a prime piece of real estate to get rid of him. This noble lover is son-in-law to the dead man, whose sheets you see airing out up there on the balcony . . . It's all a little complicated . . .

STUDENT It's damned complicated!

OLD MAN Yes, that it is, weaving in and weaving out, though it seems quite simple.

STUDENT Who was the dead man then?

OLD MAN You just asked that and I told you; if you could see around the corner, by the servant's entrance, you'd notice a bunch of poor people he helped . . . when he was in the mood . . .

STUDENT He was a charitable man, then?

OLD MAN Yes . . . sometimes.

STUDENT Not always?

OLD MAN No! . . . But that's how people are! Listen, push me a little into the sun, I'm freezing here. When you can't move, the blood numbs — I'll probably die soon, I know that, but before I do I have a few things to put in order — take my hand and feel how cold I am.

STUDENT *(Backing away)* My God!

OLD MAN Don't leave me, I'm tired, I'm alone, but I haven't always been like this, you understand; I have an endlessly long life behind me — endlessly long— I've made people unhappy and people have made me unhappy, the one pays for the other — but before I die I want to see you happy . . . Our fates are lumped together because of your father — and something more . . .

STUDENT Let go of my hand, you're draining my strength, you're freezing me to death, what do you want?

OLD MAN Patience and you shall see and understand . . . Here comes the girl . . .

STUDENT The Colonel's daughter?

OLD MAN Yes! Daughter! Look at her! — Have you ever seen such a masterpiece?

STUDENT She's like the marble statue in there . . .

OLD MAN She was her mother after all!

STUDENT You're right — "never have I seen such a woman of woman born. — Happy the man who leads her to the altar and into his home!"

OLD MAN You can see it! — Not everyone sees her beauty . . . Well, so it is written!

* * *

> *The GIRL enters from the left in modern English Amazon garb,[6] goes slowly to the door without looking at anything; there she stops and says a few words to the CONCIERGE; afterwards she goes into the house. The STUDENT covers his face with his hands.*

OLD MAN Are you crying?

STUDENT Before what is hopeless there is only despair!

OLD MAN I can open doors and hearts, as long as I find support for my will . . . Serve me and you shall rule . . .

STUDENT Is there some kind of pact? Am I to sell my soul?

OLD MAN Sell nothing! — Look, I have done nothing but *take* my whole life; now I have an urge to give! But no one will accept . . . I am rich, very rich, but have no heir, well yes, a good-for-nothing who torments the life out of me . . . become my son, be my heir while I'm still alive, enjoy the things of life so I can watch, from a distance at least.

STUDENT What do you want me to do?

OLD MAN First, go and listen to *The Valkyrie*!

STUDENT That's already decided — what more?

OLD MAN This evening you will sit in there in the Round Room!

STUDENT How will I get in there?

OLD MAN *The Valkyrie.*

STUDENT Why have you chosen me as your medium? Did you know me before?

OLD MAN Yes, of course! I have had an eye on you for a long time . . . But look there, on the balcony the maid lowers the flag to half mast for the Consul . . . and then turns the bed clothes . . . Do you see that blue quilt? — It was made for two but now there's only one . . .

The GIRL has changed her clothes and is watering the hyacinths in the window.

There is my little girl, look at her, look! — She talks to the flowers, isn't she like a blue hyacinth herself? . . . She gives them a drink, only fresh water, and they transform it into color and scent . . . now comes the Colonel with the newspaper! — He shows her the collapsed building . . . he points to your picture! She is not indifferent . . . she reads about the accident . . . I believe it's getting cloudy. What if it starts to rain and I'm stuck here, if Johansson doesn't come back soon . . .

It begins to cloud up and darken. The WHITE-HAIRED WOMAN at the gossip-mirror closes her window.

My fiancée closes her window . . . Seventy-nine years . . . the gossip-mirror is the only mirror she uses, because she can't see herself in it, only the world outside, and in two directions. But the world can see her too. She hadn't thought of that . . . A beautiful old woman all the same . . .

The DEAD MAN comes out through the door in his winding sheet.

STUDENT Good God, what's that?

OLD MAN What do you see?

STUDENT Don't you see it, at the door — the dead man?

OLD MAN I see nothing, but I expected it! Tell me . . .

STUDENT He's walking into the street...

Pause.

Now he's turning his head and looking at the flag.

OLD MAN What'd I tell you? He'll probably count the wreaths too and read the cards... Woe to anyone who's missing!

STUDENT Now he's gone around the corner...

OLD MAN He wants to count the poor at the servant's entrance... the poor add such a decorative touch to an obituary: "followed by the good wishes of the masses," yes, but my good wishes he won't have! — He was quite a racketeer, just between you and me...

STUDENT But kindly...

OLD MAN A kindly racketeer, who always looked forward to a beautiful funeral... When he felt the end approaching he bilked the government out of 50,000 crowns... now his daughter mixes herself up in another's marriage and contemplates the inheritance... he hears everything we say, the racketeer, and that can't be begrudged him! — Here comes Johansson!

JOHANSSON enters from the left.

Report!

JOHANSSON whispers to the OLD MAN.

So, not at home? You're a jackass! — And the telegram? — Nothing!... Go on!... Six o'clock this evening? That's fine! Special edition? — The whole name! Arkenholz, born... parents... excellent... I believe it's beginning to rain... What'd he say by the way?... Oh really, really! — He doesn't want to? Well, now he has to anyway! — There comes the titled gentleman! — Push me to the corner, Johansson, I want to hear what the poor are saying... And Arkenholz, wait for me here... Do you understand! — Faster, faster!

JOHANSSON pushes the chair to the corner. The STUDENT remains and watches the GIRL who digs in the flowerpots.

* * *

The BARON, dressed in mourning, talks with the LADY IN BLACK who walks along the sidewalk in front of the house.

BARON Yes, well what can we do about it? — We'll just have to wait!

LADY IN BLACK I can't wait!

BARON Is that so? Go to the countryside then!

LADY IN BLACK I don't want to.

BARON Come over here or they'll hear us.

They move over to the kiosk and continue their conversation quietly.

* * *

JOHANSSON enters from the right and speaks to the STUDENT.

JOHANSSON The boss asks that the young gentleman not forget that other matter!

STUDENT *(Slowly)* Listen — tell me first: who is he, the boss?

JOHANSSON Well! He's so many things, and he's been everything.

STUDENT Is he sane?

JOHANSSON What does that mean? — He's spent his whole life looking for a Sunday child, or so he says, but that may not be true . . .

STUDENT What does he want? Is he greedy?

JOHANSSON He wants to be in charge . . . He spends his days riding around in his chariot like the god Thor . . . he looks at houses, tears them down, widens streets, paves over market squares; but he also breaks into homes; creeps in through a window, ravages people's fate, kills his enemies and never forgives. — Can the young gentleman imagine that that little cripple was once a Don Juan, even though he always lost his women?

STUDENT That doesn't make sense.

JOHANSSON Yes, he's so demonically shrewd he gets the women to leave him when he gets tired of them . . . He's like a horse thief in the marketplace of humankind, he steals human beings, in many different ways . . . Me he literally stole from the hands of justice . . . I'd committed an indiscretion, hmm; which only he knew about; instead of throwing me in jail, he made me his retainer; I slave for room and board, which isn't even all that great . . .

STUDENT What does he want to do in that house there?

JOHANSSON Well, I can't really say! It's all so complicated.

STUDENT I think I'd better get out of here . . .

JOHANSSON Look . . .

> *The GIRL drops her bracelet through the open window; the STUDENT steps forward slowly, picks up the bracelet and hands it back to her; she thanks him stiffly; he returns to JOHANSSON.*

JOHANSSON So you're thinking of leaving . . . It's not as easy as you'd think once he gets the net over your head . . . And he fears nothing between heaven and earth . . . yes, one thing, or more precisely, one person . . .

STUDENT Wait a minute, perhaps I know!

JOHANSSON How could you know?

STUDENT A guess! — Is it . . . a little milkmaid he fears?

JOHANSSON He turns away whenever he sees a milk wagon . . . and he talks in his sleep, he must certainly have been in Hamburg once . . .

STUDENT Can he be believed, this man?

JOHANSSON You can believe him — capable of anything!

STUDENT What's he doing there around the corner?

JOHANSSON He listens to the poor . . . lacerates a little word, plucks out one stone at a time, until eventually the house falls . . . figuratively speaking, of course . . . you see, I'm an educated man and was once a book dealer . . . Will you go now?

STUDENT I have a hard time being ungrateful . . . That man once saved my father, and now he requires only a small service in return . . .

JOHANSSON What is it?

STUDENT I'm supposed to go to *The Valkyrie* . . .

JOHANSSON I don't know anything about that . . . But he always has new schemes . . . Look, now he's talking to the police . . . he always keeps in good with the police, appeals to them, involves them in his interests, binds them with false promises and future prospects, and all the time pumping them. — You'll see, before the sun goes down he'll be received into the Round Room.

STUDENT What does he want in there? What business does he have with the Colonel?

JOHANSSON Well . . . I have my suspicions, but I don't know for sure! You'll have to wait and see for yourself when you get inside! . . .

STUDENT I'll never get in there . . .

JOHANSSON That depends on you! — Go to *The Valkyrie* . . .

STUDENT Is that the way?

JOHANSSON Yes, if he said so! — Look, look at him in his war machine, pulled in triumph by the beggars, who won't get a penny out of him, only an inkling that they'll get theirs at his funeral.

> *The OLD MAN, standing in his wheel chair, is pulled by a BEGGAR, followed by others.*

OLD MAN Hail to the noble young man who put his own life in danger to rescue so many at yesterday's misfortune! Hail, Arkenholz!

> *The BEGGARS uncover their heads but do not shout. The GIRL in the window waves her handkerchief. The COLONEL stares out his window. THE OLD WOMAN rises at her window. The MAID raises the flag on the balcony to the top.*

A round of applause, fellow citizens, it is Sunday of course but the ass in the well and the corn in the field absolve us[7] and, while I am no Sunday child, I possess both the art of prophesy and the gift of healing, for I once called a drowned soul back to life . . . It was in Hamburg one Sunday morning, like today . . .

* * *

The MILKMAID enters, seen only by the STUDENT and OLD MAN; she stretches up her arms as if she were drowning and stares at the OLD MAN.

OLD MAN *(Stops suddenly and collapses in terror)* Johansson! Get me out of here! Fast! — Arkenholz, don't forget *The Valkyrie!*

STUDENT What is all this?

JOHANSSON We must wait and see! Wait and see!

The curtain falls.

2.

Inside the Round Room: on the rear wall a white tile stove with pendulum clock and candelabra; to the right, a foyer with a view into the Green Room with mahogany furniture; to the left stands the statue hidden by palms and a curtain that can be lowered to conceal it; to the left is the door into the Hyacinth Room where the GIRL sits and reads. The COLONEL can be seen from behind, writing in the Green Room. BENGTSSON, the butler, enters in livery from the foyer with JOHANSSON dressed in a tuxedo and white cravat.

BENGTSSON So you'll serve and I'll take their coats. You've done this before haven't you.

JOHANSSON By day I push the war machine, as you know, but in the evenings I'm a waiter at parties. It's always been my dream to get inside this house . . . These are strange people I'm told.

BENGTSSON We-ell, a bit uncommon, I guess you could say.

JOHANSSON Will there be a music recital or what?

BENGTSSON Just the ordinary ghost supper, as we call it. They drink tea without saying a word, or the Colonel talks by himself; and they nibble on crackers in unison so it sounds like rats in an attic.

JOHANSSON Why do you call it a ghost supper?

BENGTSSON They look like ghosts... And they've been doing this for twenty years, always the same people, who say the same things, or keep silent to avoid being shamed.

JOHANSSON Isn't there a lady of the house too?

BENGTSSON Oh yes, but that's the weirdest; she sits in a closet because her eyes can't stand the light... In fact, she's in here...

He points to a hidden door in the wall.

JOHANSSON In there?

BENGTSSON Ye-es, I said it was a bit uncommon...

JOHANSSON What does she look like?

BENGTSSON Like a mummy... Do you want to see? *(Opening the door)* See, there she sits!

JOHANSSON Sweet Jesus...

MUMMY *(Babbling)* Why'd'ja open the door? Din't I say shut it...

BENGTSSON *(Squeamishly)* Ta, ta, ta, ta! If little missy minds her manners she'll get a treat! — Pretty Polly!

MUMMY *(Like a parrot)* Pretty Polly! 'S Jacob out there? Sweeeetie!

BENGTSSON She thinks she's a parrot, and it's just possible she is... *(To the MUMMY)* Whistle a little for us, Polly.

The MUMMY whistles.

JOHANSSON I've seen a lot of things, but never the likes of this.

BENGTSSON When a house gets old it gets moldy and when people sit around torturing each other they go mad. The lady of the house — quiet Polly — this mummy has been sitting here for forty years — same husband, same furniture, same relatives, same friends... *(Closing the* *door again on the MUMMY)* And what goes on here in this house — I don't have the slightest idea . . . Look at this statue . . . it's the lady when she was young!

JOHANSSON My God! — Is that the mummy?

BENGTSSON Yes! — It brings tears to your eyes — But this woman, through the power of her imagination or something, has managed to take on the characteristics of that chatter-sick bird — she can't stand cripples or the sick . . . She can't even stand her own daughter because she's sick . . .

JOHANSSON Is the young girl sick?

BENGTSSON Didn't you know?

JOHANSSON No! ——— And the Colonel, who is he?

BENGTSSON Wait and see.

JOHANSSON *(Looking at the statue)* It's terrible to imagine . . . How old is the woman now?

BENGTSSON No one knows ——— they say when she was thirty-five she looked nineteen and convinced the Colonel she was . . . In this house . . . Do you know what that screen next to the sofa is for? — It's called a death screen. It's brought out when someone's going to die, just like in a hospital . . .

JOHANSSON This is a horrible house . . . And that student's been longing to get in here as if it were paradise . . .

BENGTSSON What student. Oh, him! The one who's coming this evening . . . The Colonel and his daughter met him at the opera and were both quite taken with him . . . Hmm! . . . But now it's my turn to ask: Who is your boss? This director in the wheel chair . . . ?

JOHANSSON Yes! Yes! — Is he coming too?

BENGTSSON He's not invited.

JOHANSSON Then he'll come uninvited! If necessary . . .

* * *

The OLD MAN appears in the foyer, dressed in a frock coat and top hat; he sneaks forward on crutches to listen.

BENGTSSON He's a real thieving jay, huh?

JOHANSSON Full-feathered.

BENGTSSON He looks like the devil himself!

JOHANSSON And a witch troll too! — He can walk through locked doors . . .

OLD MAN *(Steps forward and takes JOHANSSON by the ear)* Scoundrel — Watch yourself! *(To BENGTSSON)* Announce my visit to the Colonel!

BENGTSSON Yes, but they're expecting guests . . .

OLD MAN I know! But my visit is expected too, in a way, though not exactly anticipated . . .

BENGTSSON Oh really! What was the name? Director Hummel.

OLD MAN Precisely.

BENGTSSON goes into the Green Room closing the door behind him.

OLD MAN *(To JOHANSSON)* Vanish! *(JOHANSSON hesitates)* Vanish!

JOHANSSON disappears into the entry way. The OLD MAN inspects the room; stands in front of the statue in deep surprise.

Amalia! . . . It is her! . . . Hmm!

He strolls around the room fingering various items; he straightens his hairpiece before the mirror and returns to the statue.

MUMMY *(From inside the closet)* Pretty Polly!

OLD MAN *(To himself)* What was that? Is there a parrot in here? I don't see one!

MUMMY 'S Jacob there?

OLD MAN Must be haunted!

MUMMY Jacob!

OLD MAN Makes me nervous . . . Such secrets hidden in this house! *(Examining a painting with his back to the closet)* That's him! . . . Hmm!

MUMMY *(Coming forward behind the OLD MAN and clawing in his wig)* Sweeetie . . . 's that sweeetie?

OLD MAN *(Jumping in the air)* Holy God in heaven! — What is that?

MUMMY *(In a normal voice)* Is it you, Jacob?

OLD MAN My name is Jacob, actually . . .

MUMMY *(Meaningfully)* And my name is Amalia!

OLD MAN No, no, no . . . Lord Jesus . . .

MUMMY Yes, now I look like this — and once I looked like that! Life is so edifying — I live mostly in the closet now, to keep from having to see or to be seen . . . But you Jacob, what do you want here?

OLD MAN My child! Our child . . .

MUMMY She's in there.

OLD MAN Where?

MUMMY In the Hyacinth Room!

OLD MAN *(Looking at the GIRL)* Ah, yes!

    Pause.

What does her father say, I mean the Colonel? Your husband?

MUMMY I was angry at him once and told him everything . . .

OLD MAN Well?

MUMMY He didn't believe me. "That's what all wives say when they want to murder their husbands," he said. Still, it was a horrible crime.

His whole life is counterfeit, including his family tree; sometimes I read the Protocol of the Peers of the Realm, and then I think: that one's walking around with false identification papers just like a maid, only they're sent to the workhouse for it.

OLD MAN A lot of people do that; let me remind you that you falsified your date of birth . . .

MUMMY My mother made me . . . I can't be blamed for that! . . . But you were the guiltiest in our crime . . .

OLD MAN No, your husband instigated that crime when he took my fiancée away from me! — From birth I've been unable to forgive until I've punished — I saw it as an inescapable duty . . . and still do!

MUMMY What are you looking for in this house? What do you want? How did you get in? — Is this about my daughter? Touch her and you will die!

OLD MAN I only want what's best for her!

MUMMY You'll spare her father!

OLD MAN No!

MUMMY Then you'll die; in this very room; behind that screen . . .

OLD MAN We'll see . . . once I've clamped down on something I can't open my jaws again . . .

MUMMY You want her to marry that student: why? He's nothing. He has nothing.

OLD MAN He'll be rich, through me!

MUMMY Are you invited here this evening?

OLD MAN No, but I do expect to be invited to your little ghost supper.

MUMMY Do you know who's coming?

OLD MAN Not precisely.

MUMMY The Baron . . . who lives upstairs, and whose father-in-law was buried this morning . . .

OLD MAN The one who's getting divorced so he can marry the concierge's daughter . . . The one who was once your lover!

MUMMY And then, your former fiancée, whom my husband seduced . . .

OLD MAN A select gathering . . .

MUMMY God, if only we could die! If only we could die!

OLD MAN Why do you get together then?

MUMMY Crimes and secrets and debts bind us together! — We've split up and gone our separate ways so endlessly many times, but we're always dragged back together again . . .

OLD MAN I think the Colonel's coming . . .

MUMMY Then I'll go visit with Adèle . . .

>   *Pause.*

Jacob, think about what you're doing! Spare him . . .

>   *Pause. She goes.*

COLONEL *(Cold and reserved)* Won't you sit down.

>   *The OLD MAN sits down slowly. Pause. The COLONEL stares at the OLD MAN.*

Is it you, sir, who wrote this letter?

OLD MAN Yes.

COLONEL Your name is Hummel?

OLD MAN Yes!

>   *Pause.*

COLONEL Then I now know that you've bought up all my outstanding debts, which means my life is in your hands. What do you intend to do now?

OLD MAN To be paid, one way or another.

COLONEL What way?

OLD MAN Quite simple — let's not talk about money — only tolerate me in your home, as a guest!

COLONEL If you're served by so little . . .

OLD MAN Thank you!

COLONEL And then?

OLD MAN Fire Bengtsson!

COLONEL Why should I do that? My trusted butler — he's been with me for a generation — he received the medal of honor for faithful service to his country — why should I do that?

OLD MAN All his shining virtues are only in your imagination. — He's not what he seems to be!

COLONEL Who of us is, after all?

OLD MAN *(Shrug)* True! But Bengtsson must go!

COLONEL Will you make the decisions in my house?

OLD MAN Yes! Since I own everything here — furniture, curtains, silverware, linen cabinet . . . and more!

COLONEL What more?

OLD MAN Everything! Everything you see I own. It's all mine!

COLONEL Fine, it's yours! But my noble coat of arms and my good name remain mine!

OLD MAN No, not even that! *(Pause)* You're not really nobility!

COLONEL How dare you!

OLD MAN *(Taking out a paper)* If you would care to read this excerpt from the records you will see that the family whose name you bear died out over a hundred years ago.

COLONEL I have heard such rumors as a matter of fact, but I bear the name of my father.... *(Reads)* It's true. You're right... I am not nobility! — Not even that! — Then this signet ring — it belongs to you... Here, take it!

OLD MAN *(Putting on the ring)* To continue! — You're also not a colonel.

COLONEL Am I not?

OLD MAN No! You were temporarily appointed colonel in the American volunteer army, but after the war in Cuba and the reorganization of the army all former commissions were recalled...

COLONEL Is this true?

OLD MAN *(Taking a letter from his pocket)* Perhaps you would care to read this?

COLONEL No, it's not necessary!... Who are you who has the right to sit there and strip me bare like this?

OLD MAN That remains to be seen! Though as for stripping — do you know who you are?

COLONEL Have you no shame?

OLD MAN Take off that toupee and look in the mirror, but first take out your teeth and shave off that mustache, let Bengtsson loosen your corset, and let's see if a certain butler doesn't recognize himself: the kitchen Romeo...

The COLONEL reaches for the bell on the table.

(Anticipating) Don't touch the bell, and don't call for Bengtsson or I'll have him arrested... The guests are arriving — keep calm, and we'll play out our old roles a bit longer!

COLONEL Who are you? I recognize that look, that tone of voice...

OLD MAN Don't dig too deeply, just keep quiet and obey!

* * *

The STUDENT enters.

STUDENT *(Bowing to the COLONEL)* Herr Colonel!

COLONEL Welcome to my house, young man! Your noble behavior at yesterday's misfortune has brought your name to the lips of all, and I count it an honor to welcome you into my home . . .

STUDENT Herr Colonel, my lowly upbringing . . . Your shining name and noble heritage . . .

COLONEL May I introduce Master Arkenholz, Director Hummel . . . Perhaps I could ask you to step in and greet the ladies, while I just finish a conversation with the director . . .

The STUDENT is shown into the Hyacinth Room, where he remains visible, standing in shy conversation with the GIRL.

A superb young man, musical, he sings, writes poetry . . . If only he were of noble birth and a social equal I would have nothing against . . . yes . . .

OLD MAN Against what?

COLONEL My daughter . . .

OLD MAN *Your* daughter! — Speaking of which, why does she always sit in there?

COLONEL She must sit in the Hyacinth Room whenever she's inside! It's a quirk of hers . . . Here comes Miss Beate von Holsteinkrona . . . a charming woman . . . a member of society with an investment income sufficiently large for her social position and standing.

OLD MAN *(To himself)* My fiancée!

* * *

The WHITE-HAIRED WOMAN enters looking a bit crazy.

COLONEL Miss Holsteinkrona, Director Hummel . . .

The WHITE-HAIRED WOMAN curtsies and sits. The BARON enters furtively, dressed in mourning, and sits.

The Baron Skanskorg . . .

OLD MAN *(Acknowledging without rising)* The jewel thief I do believe. . . *(To the COLONEL)* Call in the mummy and the congregation is complete . . .

COLONEL *(At the door to the Hyacinth Room)* Polly!

* * *

MUMMY *(Entering)* Sweeetie!

COLONEL Won't the young people be joining us?

OLD MAN No! Not the young people! They're to be spared . . .

All sit in a silent circle.

*

COLONEL Shall we have tea?

OLD MAN No one here likes tea, so why pretend.

Pause.

COLONEL Perhaps you would care to converse, then?

OLD MAN *(Slowly and with pauses)* Talk about what a farce the world is, which we know; ask each other how we feel, which we know. I prefer silence, then you can hear what people think, then you can see into the past. Silence hides nothing . . . unlike words. I read the other day that the different languages actually arose among primitive peoples as an attempt to hide the secrets of the tribe from outsiders. That means that languages are ciphers, and he who finds the key can understand all the languages of the world; but that doesn't prevent secrets from being betrayed without the key, especially when it comes to proving paternity. Proving it in the courts, that's another story. There two false witnesses constitute full proof, as long as they agree. But on the kind of expeditions I'm referring to, a man takes no witnesses with him. Nature itself ordained a sense of shame among people, which serves to hide what should be kept hidden.

But we glide into situations against our will, and in time the occasion arises uninvited when the deepest secrets are made plain, then the mask is torn from the deceiver and the villain is revealed . . .

Pause. All look at one another in silence.

So very quiet all of a sudden!

Long silence.

Here for example in this respectable house, in this beautiful home where beauty, education and social position come together ———

Long silence.

All of us sitting here, we know who we are . . . don't we? . . . I don't need to say it . . . and you know me, even though you pretend not to . . . In there sits my daughter, mine, you also know that . . . She's lost the will to live without knowing why . . . She's withering in this air of exhaled crimes, deceit and falsehood . . . that's why I've searched out a friend for her in whose company she can feel the light and warmth of a noble deed . . .

Long silence.

That was my mission in this house: to dig out the weeds, expose the crimes, balance the books, so that the young might begin afresh in this house which I have given them!

Long silence.

Now I grant free passage to each and every one of you in turn; anyone who stays I'll have arrested.

Long silence.

Listen to the clock tick, like a death beetle in the wall! Do you know what it says? "Time's up! Time's up! ——— " When the clock strikes, in a few minutes, your time will be spent. Then you may go, but not before. The clock falters a moment before it strikes! — Listen! Now it warns: "The clock can strike." ——— I too can strike . . .

He strikes the table with his crutch.

Do you hear?

> *Silence.*

MUMMY *(Steps forward to the clock pendulum and stops it; then, she speaks seriously and focused)* But I can stop the race of time — I can change the past into nothing, undo what has been done, not with bribes or threats, but through suffering and remorse ——— . *(Going up to the OLD MAN)* We are pitiable people, we know that; we have sinned, we have failed, we like everyone. We are not what we seem for we are at heart better than ourselves, because we despise our faults; but that you Jacob Hummel with false name should sit and judge us, it shows that you are worse than we poor people! You are not what you seem either! — You steal human souls, you stole me once with false prospects; you murdered the consul who was buried today, you strangled him with debts; you've stolen the student by binding him with his father's supposed debt, who never owned you a penny . . .

> *The OLD MAN tries to stand and take the floor but falls back again into his chair and shrivels more and more during the MUMMY's speech.*

But there is a black spot in your life which I don't exactly know, but I suspect . . . I think Bengtsson has information about it!

> *The MUMMY rings the bell on the table.*

OLD MAN No, not Bengtsson! Not that!

MUMMY So, he does know.

> *The MUMMY rings again. The little MILKMAID appears in the doorway, unseen by everyone except the OLD MAN, who cringes. The girl disappears when BENGTSSON enters.*

MUMMY Do you know this gentleman?

BENGTSSON Yes, I know him and he knows me. Life changes as we know, and I once served in his house, another time, he served in mine. He pilfered food in my kitchen for two whole years — since he had to leave by three in the afternoon, dinner was always ready at two, and the household got to eat the warmed up leftovers when that ox had finished — he drank up the broth and replaced it with water — he sat out there like a vampire and sucked the marrow out of the house and we grew thin as skeletons — and he threatened to have us thrown in prison when we called the cook a thief. Later I met the man in Hamburg under a different name. He was a usurer, a blood sucker. And he was accused of having lured a girl out onto the ice to drown her because she had witnessed a crime that he feared would be discovered . . .

MUMMY *(Passing her hand before the OLD MAN's face)* There you are! Now take out the IOUs and loan receipts!

> *JOHANSSON watches from the foyer with great interest as he is freed from slavery. The OLD MAN takes out a bundle of papers and throws them on the table. The MUMMY slaps the OLD MAN on the back.*

Pretty Polly! 'S Jacob there?

OLD MAN *(Like a parrot)* Jacob's here! *(Squawks)* Kakadora! Dora![8]

MUMMY Can the clock strike?

OLD MAN *(Clucking)* The clock can strike! *(Imitating a cuckoo clock)* Cuckoo, cuckoo, cuckoo! ———

MUMMY *(Opening the closet door)* Now the clock has struck! — Stand up, take your place in the closet where I have sat for twenty years and wept for our forgiveness. — There's a rope in there that can take the place of the one you used to strangle the consul with, and the one you planned to strangle your benefactor with . . . Go!

> *The OLD MAN goes into the closet. The MUMMY closes the door.*

Bengtsson! Put up the screen!

> *BENGTSSON sets the screen in front of the door.*

It is consummated! — God have mercy on his soul!

ALL Amen!

> *Long silence.*

* * *

> *Inside the Hyacinth Room the GIRL can be seen at the harp,*

accompanying the STUDENT's recitation.

Song with Prelude[9]

The sun, I saw or so it seemed
I gazed upon the Hidden One;
And all his work was human joy,
Blessed is he who goodness does.
Since wrathful deeds which you have done
Cannot be cured with hate and strife;
Comfort those you have distressed
And with your goodness have you healed.
No one fears who's not done wrong;
Goodness is the innocent's crown.

Curtain

3.

A room in a somewhat bizarre style, oriental motif. Hyacinths of every color everywhere. On the mantel sits a large Buddha with a flower bulb in his lap out of which shoots a shallot with a globe-shaped center and white stars! In the back wall, to the right, is a doorway into the Round Room where the COLONEL and the MUMMY can be seen sitting still and silent; part of the death screen can also be seen; to the left, a door to the dining room and kitchen.

The STUDENT and the GIRL (Adèle) are at the table; she sits with a harp; he stands.

GIRL Sing for my flowers!

STUDENT Is this your soul's flower?

GIRL It is my one and only! Do you love hyacinths?

STUDENT I love them more than any others, their virginal bodies rising straight and slender from the bulb, resting on the water and sinking its white roots into the colorless moisture; I love their colors, the snow white innocence, the honey yellow lightness, the pink youthfulness, the red ripeness, but above all the dewy blue, the deep-eyed, the faithful ——— I love them all, more than gold or pearls, have loved them since I was a child, have adored them because they possess all the beauty I lack... However!...

GIRL What?

STUDENT My love is unrequited, for the beautiful flowers hate me...

GIRL How?

STUDENT Their sweet, strong scent, like the first breezes of spring drawn over the melting snow, swirls my senses, deafens me, dazzles me, forces me out of the room, bombards me with poison arrows, makes my heart moan and my head overheat. Do you know the flowers' song?

GIRL Tell me!

STUDENT But first their meaning. The bulb is the earth which rests on the water or lies on the clouds; now shoots the stalk straight up like the axis of the earth and on its uppermost parts sit the six-rayed star flowers.

GIRL Over the earth, the stars! How beautiful! Where did you hear it, how did you see it?

STUDENT Let me think. — In your eyes. — It is an image of the Cosmos... That's why the Buddha sits with the earth bulb, brooding with his eyes to see it grow outward and upward, transforming itself into heaven. The pitiable earth shall become heaven. That is what the Buddha waits for.

GIRL Now I see — aren't snowblossoms six-starred like the hyacinth?

STUDENT Then snowblossoms are falling stars...

GIRL And a snowdrop is a snowstar... growing out of the snow.

STUDENT And Sirius, the greatest and most beautiful of all the stars in the firmament, is yellow and red like the narcissus with its yellow and red cup and six white rays...

GIRL Have you seen the flower of a shallot?

STUDENT It bears its blossoms in a bunch, a ball that's like the globe of heaven strewn with white stars...

GIRL Yes, God, so beautiful! Whose thoughts are these?

STUDENT Yours.

GIRL Yours.

STUDENT Ours! — We have created something together, our union is consecrated . . .

GIRL Not yet . . .

STUDENT What remains?

GIRL The waiting, the testing, the patience!

STUDENT Well, test me! *(Pause)* Why do your parents sit in there in silence, without saying a word?

GIRL Because they have nothing left to say, because the one no longer believes the other. "What good is it to talk," my father would say, "when we can no longer deceive each other?"

STUDENT It's horrible . . .

GIRL There's the cook . . . Look at her, so big and fat . . .

STUDENT What does she want?

GIRL She wants to ask me about dinner. I have to take care of the household now, with mother's illness . . .

STUDENT Do we have to concern ourselves with the kitchen?

GIRL We all must eat, after all ——— The cook, I can't look at her . . .

STUDENT Who is that troll witch?

GIRL One of Hummel's vampire family. She devours us . . .

STUDENT Why don't you fire her?

GIRL She won't go! We can't touch her, she's punishment for our sins . . . don't you see that we pine away, that we are consumed . . .

STUDENT Don't you get enough to eat then?

GIRL All the energy is gone from the food we get ... She boils away the meat and gives us gristle and water while she drinks the gravy; and when she roasts, she cooks away the goodness, eats the sauce, and drinks the broth; everything she touches loses its taste. It's as if she sucked it up with her eyes; we get the grounds while she drinks the coffee, and she drinks the wine from the bottles and fills them up with water ...

STUDENT Drive her out!

GIRL We can't!

STUDENT Why not?

GIRL We don't know! She won't leave! No one can touch her — she's taken away our strength!

STUDENT Let me try?

GIRL No! It must be as it is! — Here she comes! She'll ask what we want for dinner, and I'll say this or that and she'll refuse and we'll have what she wants.

STUDENT Let her decide, then!

GIRL She won't.

STUDENT What a strange house!

GIRL Yes! — She saw you and turned away!

*

COOK *(Standing in the doorway)* No, that's not why!

> *The COOK grins so her teeth show.*

STUDENT Out, woman!

COOK When I wish! *(Pause)* Now I wish!

> *The COOK disappears.*

GIRL Don't get angry! — Practice patience; she's part of the test we undergo in this house! We also have a maid who I have to clean up after!

STUDENT I'm sinking! *Cor in æthere!* Sing!

GIRL Wait!

STUDENT Sing!

GIRL Patience — This room is called the chamber of trials — it's beautiful to look at but full of imperfections . . .

STUDENT I don't believe that. Certainly you can overlook them! It's beautiful here, but a little cold. Why don't you light the stove?

GIRL It smokes.

STUDENT Can't you clean the chimney?

GIRL It doesn't help! ——— Do you see that desk?

STUDENT Incredibly beautiful!

GIRL But it wobbles. Every day I put a piece of cork under the leg, but the maid sweeps it away and I have to cut a new one. In the morning the pen holder is covered with ink, and the pen too; I have to clean them after her, every day, rain or shine ———. *(Pause)* What is the worst thing you can think of?

STUDENT Sorting the laundry! Huu!

GIRL That's my job! Huu!

STUDENT What more?

GIRL To be awakened in the middle of the night and have to get up and fasten the shutters . . . because the maid forgot.

STUDENT What more?

GIRL To climb up on a ladder and fix the damper because the maid pulled the cord off.

STUDENT What more?

GIRL To sweep up after her, dust after her, light the stove because she only puts in the wood! To open the damper, dry the glasses, reset the table, fetch the bottles, open the windows and air out the room, remake my bed, scour the water carafe when it's green with algae, buy matches and soap which we're always out of, clean the lamps and trim the wicks so they won't smoke and fill them when we have guests so they won't go out...

STUDENT Sing!

GIRL Wait! — First the drudgery, the drudgery of keeping the filth of life away.

STUDENT But you're wealthy, you have two servants!

GIRL It doesn't help! Even if we had three! It's difficult to live and sometimes I get tired . . . Imagine if there were a nursery as well!

STUDENT The greatest of joys . . .

GIRL And the costliest ——— Is life worth so much trouble?

STUDENT That depends on what payment you expect for your labors . . . I would shun nothing to win your hand.

GIRL Don't talk like that! — You can never have me!

STUDENT Why?

GIRL You must not ask.

>   *Pause.*

STUDENT You dropped your bracelet out the window...

GIRL Because my hand had grown so thin...

>   *Pause. The* COOK *enters with a bottle of Japanese soy sauce in her hand.*

There's the one who devours me, and all of us.

STUDENT What is that she's carrying?

GIRL A bottle of food coloring, the devil's elixir, with scorpion lettering! It's the witch Madame Soya that turns water into broth, to take the place of the gravy she's eaten, to cook cabbage in or make turtle soup.

STUDENT Out!

COOK You suck the narrow out of us and we out of you, we take the blood and give you back water — with food coloring. This color! — I'm going now, but I will stay as long as I want!

>   *The COOK goes. Pause.*

STUDENT How did Bengtsson get that medal?

GIRL For faithful service to his country.

STUDENT Has he no faults?

GIRL A great many, but people don't get medals for that.

STUDENT You have many secrets here in this house . . .

GIRL Like everyone . . . let us keep ours!

>   Pause.

STUDENT Don't you like directness?

GIRL Yes, in moderation!

STUDENT Sometimes I get the urge to say everything I'm thinking; but I know the world would collapse if people were really direct. *(Pause)* I was at a funeral the other day . . . in the church — it was all very solemn and beautiful!

GIRL Director Hummel?

STUDENT My false benefactor, yes! — At the head of the casket holding the funeral mace stood a revered friend of the dearly departed. The priest impressed me particularly with his dignified air and moving words. — I cried, we all cried. — Afterwards we went to a tavern . . . there I learned that the man with the mace was in love with the son of the deceased.

> *The GIRL stares, trying to understand.*

And that the dearly departed had borrowed money from his son's admirer . . . *(Pause)* The next day, the priest was collared for embezzling church funds — a pretty affair!

GIRL Huu!

> *Pause.*

STUDENT Do you know what I think of you now?

GIRL Don't say it or I will die!

STUDENT I must or I will die! ———

GIRL It's only in the asylum that people say what's on their minds . . .

STUDENT Absolutely true! — My father ended up in a madhouse . . .

GIRL Was he sick?

STUDENT No he was quite healthy, only he was crazy! Well, it eventually slipped out one day . . . Like all of us, he was surrounded by a circle of acquaintances which for short he called friends. They were a bunch of crooks, of course, as most people are. But he needed some kind of company because he couldn't stand to be alone. Anyway, one doesn't usually tell people what one thinks of them, and he didn't either. Of course he knew how false they were deep down and how capable of treachery, but he was a prudent fellow and well brought up, so he was always polite. Then one day he gave a big dinner party — it was in the evening, he was tired after the day's work and from the strain of holding his tongue or talking the usual crap with his guests . . .

> *The GIRL cringes.*

Anyway, he rapped for silence on the table, raised his glass for a toast . . . then something came unbuttoned and in a long speech he stripped the whole company naked one by one, spelled out all their deceptions and drained himself until he was so worn out he plopped himself down in the middle of the table and told them all to go to hell!

GIRL Huu!

STUDENT I saw it all and I'll never forget what happened next! . . . My father and mother fought, the guests rushed for the door . . . and my father was taken to the madhouse where he died! *(Pause)* If you keep quiet too long stagnant water collects and things begin to rot, and that's how it is in this house too. There is something rotting here. And I thought it was paradise when I saw you go in the first time . . . I stood there on a Sunday morning looking in; I saw a colonel who was not a colonel, I had a noble benefactor who was a thief and hanged himself. I saw a mummy who lived and a young girl — speaking of which, where is virginity these days? Where is beauty? In nature and in my imagination where it is dressed in Sunday best! Where are honor and truth? In fairy tales and children's theater! Your flowers have poisoned me and I have given you poison back — I begged you to be my wife, we recited poetry, sung, and played, and then the cook came in . . . *Sursum Corda!* Try the harp again, try once more to strike from it fire and light . . . try, I beg you, I'm on my knees . . . Then I'll try it myself!

The STUDENT takes the harp but the strings give off no sound.

Dumb and deaf! The most beautiful flowers and so poisonous . . . Why won't you be my bride? Because you're sunk in life's cellar . . . the vampire in the kitchen is beginning to suck, she must be a Lamia who drains the blood from suckling children, it's always in the kitchen that a child's future is nipped in the bud, either there or in the bedroom . . . there is poison that takes away sight and poison that opens the eyes — I must have been born with the latter for I can't see the ugly as beautiful nor call evil goodness, I can not! They say Jesus descended to hell: it was his wandering on earth — this mad-house, correction-house, charnel-house earth; and the lunatics killed him when he tried to set them free, but the thief they let go because thieves always get sympathy! — Woe! Woe! upon us all. Savior of the world, save us, we perish!

The GIRL sinks down, seems to be dying, rings. BENGTSSON enters.

GIRL Bring the screen! Quickly—I am dying!

BENGTSSON returns with the screen which he opens and sets in front of the GIRL.

STUDENT Come, freedom-giver! Welcome, you pale, mild one!—Sleep beautiful child, unhappy, innocent, guiltless in your suffering, sleep without dreams, and when you wake again . . . may you be greeted by a sun that does not burn, in a home without dust, by friends without shame and love without faults ——— You wise, mild Buddha, who sits there and waits for heaven to grow up out of the earth, loan us patience during the trials, and purity of will, so that hope will not come to shame!

The harp's strings begin to murmur; the room fills with white light.

The sun I saw, or so it seemed
I gazed upon the Hidden One;
And all his work was human joy,
Blessed is he who goodness does.
Since wrathful deeds which you have done
Cannot be cured with hate and strife;
Comfort those you have distressed
And with your goodness have you healed.
No one fears who's not done wrong
Goodness is the innocent's crown.

A moaning is heard from behind the screen.

Poor little child, child of this willful, debt-riddled, suffering and dying world; this ever changing, miscalculating and painful world! Father in Heaven bless thee on thy journey . . .

The room disappears; Böcklin's painting "The Island of the Dead"[10] becomes visible in the background; soft music, calm, enchanting and sad, can be heard coming from the island.

The Pelican

Opus 4 of the Chamber Plays (1907)

The Pelican

Characters

THE MOTHER, Elise, a widow.
THE SON, Fredrik, a law student.
THE DAUGHTER, Gerda.
THE SON-IN-LAW, Axel, married to Gerda.
MARGRET, a servant.

1.

A sitting room. Door in the rear wall to the dining room; to the right, a portion of the balcony door. A large bureau with writing desk, a chaise longue with purplish red cover; a rocking chair.

THE MOTHER, dressed in mourning clothes, sits idly in a chair. Now and then she seems to listen nervously. In another room someone plays Chopin's Fantaisie Impromptu, Oeuvre Posthume, op. 66.

MARGRET, the cook, enters from the door in the rear wall.

MOTHER Close the door, please.

MARGRET Is Madam alone?

MOTHER Close the door, please. — Who's that playing?

MARGRET Such dreadful weather this evening, rain and wind . . .

MOTHER Close the door, will you please. Spruce twigs and carbolic acid . . . I can't stand the smell . . .

MARGRET I know. That's why I said he should be taken out to the cemetery right away . . .

MOTHER The children, they wanted the funeral at home . . .

MARGRET Why do you stay here? Why don't you move someplace else?

MOTHER The landlord won't let us, we're stuck here . . . *(Pause)* Why did you take the cover off the sofa?

MARGRET I had to send it to be cleaned. *(Pause)* You know he drew his last breath on that sofa; but, take it away then . . .

MOTHER I can't touch a thing before the inventory is finished . . . I'm shut up here . . . and I can't be in the other room . . .

MARGRET Why not?

MOTHER Memories . . . all unpleasant, and that awful smell . . . Is that my son playing?

MARGRET Yes. He's unhappy here; tense; and hungry, always hungry. Says he's never had enough to eat . . .

MOTHER He was always delicate, since the day he was born . . .

MARGRET A bottle-fed baby needs healthy food once it's weaned . . .

MOTHER *(Sharply)* Well? Has anything been lacking?

MARGRET Not exactly, but still, you shouldn't have always bought the cheapest and the worst; and sending a child to school on a cup of chicory and a piece of bread, it's not right.

MOTHER My children have never complained about the food . . .

MARGRET Oh no? Well not to you, anyway, they wouldn't dare, but as they grew up, they came to me in the kitchen . . .

MOTHER We've always had limited means . . .

MARGRET I read in the newspaper that your husband paid taxes on as much as 20,000 crowns some years . . .

MOTHER It just disappeared!

MARGRET And the children are so weak. Look at poor Miss Gerda, I mean, the young thing's nearly twenty and she hasn't sprouted yet . . .

MOTHER Such talk.

MARGRET Yes, yes. *(Pause)* Wouldn't you like me to light the stove for you? It's cold in here.

MOTHER No thank you. We don't have money to burn . . .

MARGRET But the boy's forever freezing, so he has to go out or play to keep warm . . .

MOTHER He's always been cold . . .

MARGRET Why's that, do you suppose?

MOTHER Watch yourself, Margret . . . *(Pause)* Is there someone out there?

MARGRET No, no one . . .

MOTHER Do you think I'm afraid of ghosts?

MARGRET How would I know — — — But I'm not staying on here much longer . . . When I first came here it was like I'd been convicted, sentenced to watch over the children . . . I wanted to leave when I saw how the servants were treated but I couldn't, like I wasn't allowed . . . Now that Miss Gerda is married it seems like I've served my time and soon I'll be up for parole. Not quite yet, but soon . . .

MOTHER I don't understand a word you're saying — the whole world knows how I've offered myself for my children, how I've cared for my house and my duties . . . You're the only one accusing me, but see if I care. You're free to go whenever you want. I don't intend to keep any servants anymore anyway, once the young couple moves in . . .

MARGRET Well, I wish you the best of luck . . . children aren't very appreciative by nature, and a mother-in-law's not a pleasant sight, unless of course she brings money with her . . .

MOTHER Don't worry . . . I'll pay my own way, and lend a hand in the house . . . besides, my son-in-law is different . . .

MARGRET Is he?

MOTHER Yes, he is! He doesn't treat me like a mother-in-law, more like a sister, or a friend... *(Margret smirks)* I saw that. I like my son-in-law, I have the right, and he deserves it... my husband didn't like him. He was envious, jealous even. Yes, he honored me with his jealousy even though I'm not as young as I once was... Did you say something?

MARGRET Nothing! — But I do think I heard something... Probably just the boy coughing. Maybe I should light a fire.

MOTHER It's not necessary!

MARGRET Madam! — I have frozen and starved in this house, and that doesn't matter, but give me a proper bed, I am old and tired...

MOTHER Now? It's a bit late when you're all set to leave...

MARGRET True! I forgot that! But for the honor of the house, burn my sheets. People have died in them. At least burn the sheets so you can face whoever comes after me without shame. If anyone will come.

MOTHER No one's going to come!

MARGRET And if someone does, she won't stay... I've seen fifty maids come and go...

MOTHER Because they were bad people, you all are...

MARGRET Well thank you! — — — Now it'll be your turn! Each one in turn, from first to last!

MOTHER Have I had enough of you soon?

MARGRET Yes, soon! Very soon! Sooner than you think.

MARGRET exits.

* * *

The SON enters with a book, coughing. He stammers slightly.

MOTHER Close the door, please.

SON Why?

MOTHER Is that how you answer your mother? — What do you want?

SON May I sit in here and read? It's so cold in my room.

MOTHER Oh, you're always cold.

SON When you sit still, you feel it more. *(Pause, pretends to read)* Is the inventory ready yet?

MOTHER What a question. Can't we at least observe a decent period of mourning first. Don't you grieve your father?

SON Yes ... but — he's probably better off. — I don't begrudge him the peace he's found at last. But that doesn't stop me wanting to know how things stand for me — if I'll be able to finish my exams without having to borrow money ...

MOTHER Your father left nothing, you know that, maybe some debts ...

SON The business is worth something—?

MOTHER Don't you understand, there is no business, no goods, no merchandise ...

SON *(Thinking)* The firm, the name, the customers ...

MOTHER You can't sell customers ...

    Pause.

SON I've heard you can.

MOTHER Have you been to see a lawyer? *(Pause)* Is that how you mourn your father?

SON No, not really. — But first things first. — Where are my sister and her husband?

MOTHER They came home from their honeymoon this morning and are staying at some cheap hotel.

SON Well, at least they'll get enough to eat.

MOTHER Food — that's all you ever talk about. Have you had anything to complain about?

SON No, of course not.

MOTHER Tell me something. A while ago, you remember, when I was forced to live . . . separated from your father for a while, you were alone with him — did he ever talk about his business affairs?

SON *(Engrossed in his book)* Nothing special!

MOTHER Can you explain how he left nothing when he earned 20,000 crowns last year?

SON I don't know anything about father's affairs; but he said the household cost a lot, and then there was this new furniture.

MOTHER He said that, did he? Do you think he had any debts?

SON I don't know. He had some but they were paid back.

MOTHER Where did the money go? Did he leave a will? He hated me, and several times threatened to leave me without a roof over my head. Is it possible he hid his savings somewhere? *(Pause)* Is there someone out there?

SON I didn't hear anything.

MOTHER I'm a little nervous . . . all this business about money and the funeral and everything. — Anyway, you know your sister and brother-in-law are going to take this apartment now, and you'll have to find a room in town.

SON I know.

MOTHER Don't you like your brother-in-law?

SON Nothing in common.

MOTHER But he's a good fellow, and bright! — You should like him, he deserves it.

SON He doesn't like me much either — and besides, he behaved terribly towards father.

MOTHER Whose fault was that?

SON Father was no terror . . .

MOTHER No?

SON You know, I think I do hear someone out there.

MOTHER Put on a light! But just one *(The SON turns on an electric lamp, pause)* Would you like to take your father's portrait into your room? The one on the wall?

SON Why?

MOTHER I don't like it. The eyes are so terrible.

SON I don't think so.

MOTHER Take it, then, if you value it so much . . .

SON *(Taking the portrait)* I will.

> Pause.

MOTHER I'm expecting Axel and Gerda . . . do you want to see them?

SON I'm in no hurry . . . I'll stay in my room . . . if I can have a little firewood for the stove.

MOTHER We don't have money to burn . . .

SON For twenty years we've heard that, though there was always money for idiotic trips abroad . . . or to eat in fancy restaurants — a hundred crowns on one meal — that's four cords of firewood! Four cords on one meal!

MOTHER Such talk.

SON Yes, there was something crazy, but that's finished now . . . only the settlement left . . .

MOTHER What is that supposed to mean?

SON The inventory . . . and the other . . .

MOTHER What other?

SON Debts and unsettled business . . .

MOTHER I see.

SON Anyway, can I have some money for a new sweater?

MOTHER How can you ask that now? You should be thinking about earning a little money of your own soon . . .

SON When I've finished my exams.

MOTHER You could borrow like everyone else.

SON Who would loan me money?

MOTHER Your father's friends.

SON He had no friends. An independent man can't have friends, since friendship means binding yourself to mutual admiration . . .

MOTHER How wise, you learned that from your father.

SON Yes, he was a wise man — who acted foolishly sometimes.

MOTHER Now just a minute! — Well, don't you plan to get married?

SON No thank you. Keep a companion for the young men; be legal guardian for a coquette; arm your best friend, that is to say your worst enemy, to wage war against you . . . No, I watch out for myself!

MOTHER What am I hearing? — Go to your room. I've had just about enough for one day. Have you been drinking?

SON I always have to drink a little, for the cough, and to feel as if I've eaten something.

MOTHER So, there's something wrong with the food again?

SON Nothing wrong, only it's so light it tastes like air.

MOTHER *(Astonished)* You may go!

SON Or there's so much pepper and salt it makes you even hungrier — spicy air!

MOTHER You're drunk! Get out of here.

SON Sure . . . I'll go. There was one more thing, but that'll do for today. — Yes! *(Goes)*

* * *

> The MOTHER paces worried. She opens and closes the desk drawers.

*

> The SON-IN-LAW enters hastily.

MOTHER At last! Here you are, Axel. I've missed you, but where's Gerda?

SON-IN-LAW She'll be along later. How are you, how are things here?

MOTHER Sit down and let me ask first. We haven't seen each other since the wedding. — Why did you come home so soon? You were supposed to be away eight days and it's only been three.

SON-IN-LAW Yes, well, it was so long, you know, when you've talked yourself out, the loneliness become oppressive, and we were so used to your company that we missed you.

MOTHER Really? Well, we three have stuck together through all the storms and I think I can say I've been of some help to you two.

SON-IN-LAW Gerda is a child. She doesn't understand the art of living. Prejudiced and a little obstinate, fanatic in some cases. . .

MOTHER Well, now, what did you think of the wedding?

SON-IN-LAW Particularly successful. Particularly. And the verses, what did you think of them?

MOTHER The poem to me, do you mean? Ah, yes, never has a mother-in-law received such verses at her daughter's wedding . . . Remember the lines about the pelican who gives her blood for her young, I cried, you know . . . I cried . . .

SON-IN-LAW At first, yes, but then you danced every dance. Gerda was almost jealous of you . . .

MOTHER Oh, it's not the first time; she wanted me to wear black, can you imagine, out of respect, she said. But I paid no attention to her; should I obey my young?

SON-IN-LAW Don't you worry about that. Gerda can be silly sometimes, if I so much as look at another woman . . .

MOTHER What? Aren't you happy?

SON-IN-LAW Happy? Yes, what is that?

MOTHER So? Have you quarreled already?

SON-IN-LAW Already? We've done nothing else since we were engaged . . . And now this, I have to resign my commission and join the reserves . . . It's strange, but it's as if she likes me less as a civilian . . .

MOTHER Why don't you wear your uniform then? I must admit I hardly recognize you in civilian clothes — you really are another person . . .

SON-IN-LAW I'm not allowed to wear my uniform except on duty or parade . . .

MOTHER Not allowed?

SON-IN-LAW Orders.

MOTHER What a shame, for Gerda anyway; she was engaged to a lieutenant and now she's married to a bookkeeper!

SON-IN-LAW What can you do about it? Have to live! A propos of living, how's this business shaping up?

MOTHER Honestly, I just don't know. But I'm beginning to suspect Fredrik.

SON-IN-LAW How so?

MOTHER He talked so strangely this afternoon . . .

SON-IN-LAW That sheep-head . . .

MOTHER They can be insidiously sly, and I'm not sure there's not a will here somewhere or some savings maybe . . .

SON-IN-LAW Have you investigated?

MOTHER I've searched all his drawers . . .

SON-IN-LAW The boy's?

MOTHER Of course, and his wastepaper basket. I always go through that, he writes letters that he later tears up . . .

SON-IN-LAW It's nothing. But have you searched the old man's desk?

MOTHER Naturally . . .

SON-IN-LAW Thoroughly? All the drawers?

MOTHER All!

SON-IN-LAW There are usually secret drawers in every desk.

MOTHER I didn't think of that.

SON-IN-LAW We must investigate then.

MOTHER No, don't touch it, it's sealed for the inventory.

SON-IN-LAW Can't you get around the seal?

MOTHER No. It's impossible!

SON-IN-LAW Sure, if you loosen the boards in the back. Secret drawers are always in the back . . .

MOTHER You need tools for that . . .

SON-IN-LAW No, it's coming loose . . .

MOTHER But Gerda mustn't know.

SON-IN-LAW Naturally — — she'd only run to her dear brother . . .

MOTHER *(Closing the door)* I'll just close the door for safety's sake . . .

SON-IN-LAW *(Examining the back of the desk)* Someone's been in here . . . the back is loose . . . I can slip my hand in . . .

MOTHER The boy . . . You see, my suspicions . . . Hurry, someone's coming!

SON-IN-LAW A paper . . .

MOTHER Hurry . . . someone's coming . . .

SON-IN-LAW An envelope . . .

MOTHER It's Gerda. Give it to me . . . quick!

SON-IN-LAW *(Handing the MOTHER a large envelop, which she hides)* Hide it!

* * *

The door knob turns, then there's a pounding at the door.

SON-IN-LAW Why did you lock the door? — We're lost.

MOTHER Quiet!

SON-IN-LAW You fool — — — Open it! — Or I will! — Get out of the way!

He opens the door.

GERDA *(Entering, troubled)* Why did you lock yourselves in?

MOTHER Don't you even say hello, child? I haven't seen you since the wedding. How was your trip? Now, tell me all about it. And don't look so gloomy.

GERDA *(Sits in a chair, dejected)* Why did you lock the door?

MOTHER Because it keeps blowing open by itself, and I'm tired of nagging every time someone comes in. Shall we think about furnishing your apartment now? You will be living here, won't you?

GERDA I guess we must — — — it doesn't matter to me — what does Axel say?

SON-IN-LAW It'll be fine here and your mother won't have it so bad . . . since we all get along . . .

GERDA Where will mamma sleep?

MOTHER In here, my child, I'll just bring in a bed.

SON-IN-LAW In the sitting room, my dear?

GERDA Who? Me?

SON-IN-LAW I meant . . . but that'll work itself out . . . we'll have to help one another now, and with what she pays, we can manage . . .

GERDA (*Brightening*) And I'll have a little help with the housekeeping . . .

MOTHER Of course, my child . . . but I won't wash the dishes.

GERDA Don't even think of it. As for the rest, this will be fine, as long as I can have my man to myself. They can't so much as look at him . . . They did, you know, back at the hotel, and that's why the trip was so short . . . But anyone who tries to take him is dead! So now we know —

MOTHER Now, let's go out and start arranging the furniture . . .

SON-IN-LAW (*Catching the MOTHER's eye*) Good! Gerda can begin in here . . .

GERDA Why? I don't want to be left alone in here . . . I won't feel right until we've really moved in . . .

SON-IN-LAW If you're afraid of the dark, we'll all go . . .

> All three exit.

* * *

> *The room is empty. A wind blows up outside. It shrieks in the windows and in the stove; the rear door begins to bang, papers from the desk fly around the room, a palm bristles furiously, a photograph falls from the wall. The son is heard: "Mamma." Immediately afterwards: "Close the window!"*

Pause. The rocking chair rocks on its own. The MOTHER enters hastily with a paper, which she reads.

MOTHER What is this? The rocking chair's moving by itself!

The SON-IN-LAW enters.

SON-IN-LAW What was it? What does it say? Let me read. Is it a will?

MOTHER Close the door! We'll blow away. God the smell, open a window. It's not a will — it's a letter to the boy, full of lies about me — and you.

SON-IN-LAW Let me see.

MOTHER No, it will only poison you, I'll rip it to bits. Luckily it didn't fall into his hands.

She tears up the letter and throws it into the stove.

Just imagine, rising to speak from the grave — he's not dead! I can never live here. — He writes that I murdered him . . . I didn't! He died of a stroke, the doctor said so . . . but there's more, all lies! That I ruined him! . . . Listen, Axel, promise me we'll get out of this place soon, I can't take it here! Promise me — Look at the rocking chair!

SON-IN-LAW A draft . . .

MOTHER We have to get out of here. Promise me.

SON-IN-LAW I can't . . . I was counting on the inheritance, since you waved it in front of me, otherwise I'd never have married. Now we have to take things as they are, and you can consider me a duped in-law — and ruined. We must stick together to survive. That means cutting costs and you must help.

MOTHER You mean I'm to be employed as a maid in my own home? I won't.

SON-IN-LAW Necessity dictates . . .

MOTHER You scoundrel.

SON-IN-LAW Behave yourself, my dear!

MOTHER A maid, to you!

SON-IN-LAW Think how your maids have had it, starving, freezing. At least you'll be better off than they were.

MOTHER I have my annuity . . .

SON-IN-LAW It's not enough for a room in an attic, but here it'll help pay the rent, if we sit tight . . . and if you don't sit tight, I leave.

MOTHER Leave Gerda? You've never loved her . . .

SON-IN-LAW You know that better than I . . . You rooted her out of my thoughts, pushed her aside except in the bedroom. That she got to keep . . . and if there were to be a child, you'd take that too . . . She knows nothing yet, understands nothing, but she's beginning to wake up from her sleepwalking. When she opens her eyes, watch out.

MOTHER Axel! We must stick together . . . We can't be separated . . . I can't live alone. I'll accept anything — but not the sofa . . .

SON-IN-LAW I don't want to spoil the place with a bed in here — that's final.

MOTHER Let me get another one . . .

SON-IN-LAW We don't have money for that, and besides, it's quite nice.

MOTHER It looks like a bloody butcher's block.

SON-IN-LAW Such talk . . . But if you don't want it, there's always the attic and loneliness, charity and the poorhouse.

MOTHER I accept.

SON-IN-LAW As you should . . .

Pause.

MOTHER Imagine, he wrote to his son that he was murdered.

SON-IN-LAW There are many ways to murder . . . and your way had the advantage of falling outside the penal code.

MOTHER Say our way! You helped, the way you tormented him into a fury and drove him to despair . . .

SON-IN-LAW He stood in the way and wouldn't bow out, so I had to push him a little . . .

MOTHER The only thing I hold against you is that you lured me away from the home . . . I can't forget that evening, the first in your place, when we sat down to that lovely meal and heard those awful shouts from the fields below. We thought they came from the prison yard or the madhouse . . . do you remember? It was him in the tobacco barn in the dark and the rain, whimpering, longing for his wife and children . . .

SON-IN-LAW Why talk about that now? How do you even know it was him?

MOTHER It said so in his letter.

SON-IN-LAW So, what difference does it make? He was no angel . . .

MOTHER No he wasn't, but he had human feelings sometimes, yes, a little more than you . . .

SON-IN-LAW Your sympathies begin to turn . . .

MOTHER Don't be angry. We must keep peace.

SON-IN-LAW We must. We're doomed. . .

> *Hoarse cries from within.*

MOTHER What was that? Did you hear? It was him . . .

SON-IN-LAW *(Brutally)* Which one?

> *The MOTHER listens.*

Who is it? — The boy! He's been drinking again.

MOTHER Fredrik? It was so like him — I thought — — — I can't stand it. What's wrong with him?

SON-IN-LAW Go have a look. The good-for-nothing's drunk.

MOTHER How dare you! He is my son, after all.

SON-IN-LAW *(Looks at his watch)* Yes, after all, your son.

MOTHER Why are you looking at your watch? Aren't you staying for supper?

SON-IN-LAW No thank you, I don't drink tea water and I never eat rancid anchovies . . . or porridge . . . besides, I have an appointment . . .

MOTHER What kind of appointment?

SON-IN-LAW Business, that doesn't concern you. You're not going to start behaving like a mother-in-law, are you?

MOTHER You're not going to leave your wife on her first evening home?

SON-IN-LAW That's none of your business either! — — —

MOTHER I begin to see what lies ahead for me — and my children. Now comes the unmasking.

SON-IN-LAW Yes. Now it comes.

Curtain falls.

2.

The same set. In another room someone plays Godard's Bercuse de Jocelyn.[1] *GERDA sits at the desk.*

A long pause. The SON enters.

SON Are you alone?

GERDA Yes. Mamma is in the kitchen.

SON Where's Axel?

GERDA He had an appointment . . . Sit down and talk to me, Fredrik, keep me company.

SON *(Sitting)* I don't think we've ever spoken before, we avoid each other. Nothing in common.

GERDA You always sided with father, and I with mother.

SON Maybe that will change now. — Did you know father?

GERDA What a strange question! But I saw him really only through mother's eyes . . .

SON You saw how fond he was of you.

GERDA Then why did he want to break off my engagement?

SON Because he didn't think your husband was the kind of support you needed.

GERDA And he was punished for it too, when mamma left him.

SON Was that your husband's doing?

GERDA His and mine. Father was to find out how it felt to be separated, since he wanted to separate me from my fiancé.

SON Anyway, it shortened his life . . . And believe me, he only wanted the best for you.

GERDA You stayed with him. What did he say? How did he take it?

SON A misery I can't describe . . .

GERDA What did he say about mamma?

SON Nothing! . . . Anyway, after all I've seen, I'm never getting married. *(Pause)* Are you happy, Gerda?

GERDA Yes! When you've got what you've always wanted, you're happy.

SON Why did your husband leave you on your first evening home?

GERDA He had business, an appointment.

SON At a restaurant?

GERDA What?

SON I thought you knew.

GERDA Oh God, oh God!

SON I'm sorry, I didn't mean to hurt you.

GERDA So much hurt. I think I'm going to die.

SON Why didn't you stay longer on your honeymoon?

GERDA He was worried about business and he missed mamma, he can't be away from her . . .

    They stare at one another.

SON Oh. *(Pause)* Did you have a nice trip otherwise?

GERDA Yes.

SON Poor Gerda.

GERDA What do you mean?

SON You know how curious mother can be, and she can use the telephone better than anyone.

GERDA What? Has she been spying?

SON Always . . . She's probably listening behind the door right now . . .

GERDA You always think the worst of mother . . .

SON And you, always the best. How can that be? You know how she is . . .

GERDA No. I don't want to hear it . . .

SON There's more you don't want — .

GERDA Don't. I'm sleepwalking, I know, but I don't want to wake up. Then I couldn't go on living.

SON Don't you know we're all sleepwalking? — As a law student I've been reading about great criminals who can't explain how it happened . . . They thought they were behaving properly, right up until they were apprehended and woke up! If it's not a dream, it's at least a kind of sleep.

GERDA Let me sleep. I know I'll wake up, but not yet, not for a long time. All this, so much I don't really know, but can sense! Remember as children . . . people said you were bad if you told the truth . . . wicked little mind, they said, and all I did was tell the truth . . . so I learned to keep quiet . . . and everyone said, she's so well behaved; and I learned to say things I didn't mean, and then I was ready to go out into life.

SON It's true one should overlook the faults and weaknesses of others . . . but the next step is empty flattery. It's hard to know how to behave . . . sometimes it's a duty to speak . . .

GERDA Shhh!

SON I'll be quiet

    Pause.

GERDA No, I'd rather you talked, but not about that. I hear your thoughts in the silence . . . when people get together, they talk, endlessly, to hide their thoughts . . . to forget, to deafen themselves . . . They want to hear news about others, but conceal their own.

SON Poor Gerda!

GERDA Do you know what hurts most? — *(Pause)* Finding out how empty your secret longings can be.

SON It's so true.

GERDA Let's have a fire. I'm freezing.

SON Are you cold too?

GERDA I'm always frozen and hungry.

SON You too. It's strange, this house. — But if I go for wood there'll be hell to pay.

GERDA Maybe there's some there already. Mamma sometimes prepares a fire . . . to fool us . . .

> *The SON goes to the stove and opens the door.*

SON There are a few sticks in here. *(Pause)* What's this? — A letter! Ripped up. It will start a good fire . . .

GERDA Fredrik, don't. We'll just start trouble that will never end. Come and sit down again and we'll talk . . .

> *The SON sits, setting the letter on the table next to him. Pause.*

GERDA Do you know why father hated my husband so much?

SON Your Axel came and took his daughter and his wife away, and he was left alone; and then the old man noticed that someone ate better than he did; you locked yourselves in here and played music and read books, but always things that he hated. He was closed out, starved out of his own home and that's why he went out to bars in the end.

GERDA We didn't think about what we were doing . . . Poor father! — It's good to have parents with an unimpeachable name and reputation, and we can be grateful . . . Remember their silver anniversary? The speeches and the beautiful verses.

SON I remember, and I think it was quite a spectacle — honoring a happy marriage, that was really a dog's life . . .

GERDA Fredrik!
SON I can't help it. You know how they lived . . . don't you remember

when mamma tried to jump out the window and we had to hold her back.

GERDA Shhhh . . .

SON There were reasons we didn't know . . . And during the separation, when I was with the old man, it's like several times he wanted to speak, but the words stuck on his lips . . . I dream about him sometimes . . .

GERDA So do I — and when I see him then he's thirty . . . he turns to me, so kindly, but I can't understand what he's wants . . . and sometimes mamma is there too, and she's not mad at him because he loves her despite everything. You remember how beautifully he spoke to her at the anniversary, thanked her, despite everything . . .

SON Despite everything. So much to say and still so little.

GERDA It was so beautiful. And she did deserve it . . . the way she cared for the home.

SON Yes, there's the big question.

GERDA What do you mean?

SON You see how you stick together. One little word about the housekeeping and you're all back on the same side . . . like freemasons or the Camorra[2] . . . I've asked dear old Margret, who's my friend, about the household economy, I've asked her why we never feel like we eat in this house . . . She just shuts up, the old chatterbox . . . shuts up and is hurt . . . Can you explain that?

GERDA No.

SON Sounds like you're one of the freemasons too.

GERDA I don't understand what you mean.

SON Sometimes I wonder if father was a victim of this Camorra, which he must have discovererd . . .

GERDA Sometimes you talk like an idiot . . .

SON I remember he used the word Camorra sometimes, as a joke, but in the end, he kept quiet.

GERDA It's terrible how cold it is here, cold as a grave . . .

SON I'm going to light the fire, who cares what it costs.

> *The SON picks up the torn letter, casually at first, but then he begins to read.*

What is this? *(Pause)* "To my Son"! . . . It's father's handwriting! *(Pause)* And it's to me!

> *He reads, falls onto a chair and continues reading in silence.*

GERDA What are you reading? What is it?

SON It's terrible . . . *(Pause)* Awful!

GERDA Tell me, what is it?

> *Pause.*

SON This is too much . . . *(To GERDA)* It's a letter from my dead father to me. *(Continues reading)* Now I am awaking from my sleep.

> *He throws himself onto the sofa and bellows in pain, stuffing the paper into his pocket.*

GERDA *(On her knees next to the SON)* What is it Fredrik? Tell me, what is it? — Little brother, are you ill? Tell me.

SON I can't go on living.

GERDA Tell me.

SON This is all too unbelievable! . . .

> *Gathering himself together, the SON stands up.*

GERDA Maybe it's not true.

SON *(Irritated)* No, he doesn't lie, not from the grave . . .

GERDA Sometimes he was haunted by sickly imaginings . . .

SON Camorra! Are you here again; then I will tell you — — and you will listen!

GERDA I feel as if I know it already; but I still won't believe it.

SON You don't want to! — However, it's like this. She who gave us life is the mastermind.

GERDA No.

SON She stole the household money, doctored the accounts, bought the worst stuff at the highest prices; she ate in the kitchen in the morning and gave us watered down leftovers; she skimmed the cream off the milk, that's why we're miserable children, always sick and hungry; she stole the wood money and we froze. When our father found out, he warned her and she promised to change, but continued on with new discoveries: soy sauce and cayenne pepper.

GERDA I don't believe a word of it.

SON Camorra!— But now comes the worst. That slime who's now your husband, Gerda, he's never loved you. He loves your mother .

GERDA Hu!

SON When father discovered this and when your husband borrowed money from her, your mother, our mother, the crook changed his game and proposed to you. That's the main plot, you can work out the details for yourself.

GERDA (*Crying into her handkerchief*) I knew it all before, yet I didn't know it . . . it wouldn't sink in, it was too much.

SON And what can be done now to save you from disgrace?

GERDA Follow along —

SON Where?

GERDA Don't know

SON So, wait and see how things develop.

GERDA We are defenseless against our own mother, a mother is holy . . .

SON Like hell!

GERDA Don't say that.

SON She's a cunning animal, but so full of herself she's blind . . .

GERDA Let's get away!

SON Where? No, stay until that crook drives her from the house. — Quiet, the crook's home. — Quiet! — Gerda, we'll have our own secrets from now on, and the password: "he struck you on your wedding night."

GERDA Remind me often of that or I will forget! So gladly forget!

SON Our life is destroyed . . . nothing sacred, nothing to look up to . . . can't forget . . . let's live to exonerate ourselves, and our father's memory!

GERDA And see justice done!

SON Say vengeance!

* * *

AXEL enters.

GERDA *(Acting)* Hello there—How was your appointment? Did you have something good?

SON-IN-LAW It was cancelled.

GERDA Did you say closed?

SON-IN-LAW I said cancelled.

GERDA Well, are you here to take over the household then?

SON-IN-LAW You're in good humor this evening, but then Fredrik is such good company.

GERDA We've been playing freemasons.

SON-IN-LAW A dangerous game.

SON Then let's play Camorra instead. Or how about vendetta!

SON-IN-LAW *(Uneasy)* You're talking so strangely, what's going on? Some secret?

GERDA You're not telling your secrets, am I right? But maybe you don't have any.

SON-IN-LAW What's been going on? Has someone been here?

SON Gerda and I have had a séance. We've had a visitor from beyond.

SON-IN-LAW Let's stop with this game now, before things turn nasty. Though I must admit, the smile does suit you, Gerda. You're always sulking.

> *The SON-IN-LAW tries to kiss GERDA on the cheek but she pulls away.*

Are you afraid of me?

GERDA Not at all! There are emotions that seem like fear but are something else, just as there are gestures that say more than expressions, and words that conceal what neither gestures nor expressions can reveal . . .

> *The SON-IN-LAW thumbs through a book on the shelf. The SON gets up from the rocking chair, which continues to rock.*

SON Here comes mother with the porridge!

SON-IN-LAW Is it . . .

* * *

MOTHER *(Entering, is startled to see the rocking chair moving but steadies herself)* Come have some porridge.

SON-IN-LAW No thank you. If it's oats give it to the dogs, if you have any, and if it's rye put it on your boils . . .

MOTHER We're poor and have to cut costs . . .

SON-IN-LAW 20,000 a year is not poor.

SON It is if you lend to people who don't pay back.

SON-IN-LAW What is this? Is the boy crazy?

SON Maybe he has been.

MOTHER Are you coming?

GERDA Come, gentlemen. Take heart, I have steaks with bread and butter . . .

MOTHER Have you?

GERDA I do, in my house . . .

MOTHER Just imagine!

GERDA *(Gesturing toward the door)* This way, gentleman.

SON-IN-LAW *(To the MOTHER)* What's going on here?

MOTHER An owl's in the fields.

SON-IN-LAW I believe it! —

GERDA Gentleman, if you will.

All move toward the door.

MOTHER Did you see the rocking chair moving by itself? His rocking chair.

SON-IN-LAW No, I didn't see that. But I saw other things.

Curtain.

3.

Same set. In another room someone plays the waltz "Il me disait" *by Ferraris. GERDA sits with a book.*

MOTHER *(Entering)* Recognize it?

GERDA The waltz? Yes.

MOTHER Your wedding waltz. I danced it right through till morning.

GERDA You? – Where's Axel?

MOTHER What do I care?

GERDA So . . . Quarreled already?

Pause.

MOTHER What are you reading, little one?

GERDA The cookbook. Why doesn't it say how long things are supposed to be cooked?

MOTHER *(Embarrassed)* It varies so much, you see, people have different tastes, some do things this way, some that . . .

GERDA I don't understand; food should be served when it's ready, otherwise it's just warmed up, which means ruined. Yesterday for example you cooked a grouse for three hours; after the first hour the whole apartment was filled with the most wonderful aroma; then it got very quiet in the kitchen; and when the food was served the aroma was gone and it tasted like air. Explain that?

MOTHER *(Embarrassed)* I don't understand.

GERDA Explain then why there was no gravy — . Where did that disappear?

MOTHER I don't understand anything.

GERDA Well, I've asked myself a few things and I've found out a good deal . . .

MOTHER Nothing I don't already know. You won't teach me anything new, but I'll teach you about the art of housekeeping . . .

GERDA You mean soy sauce and cayenne pepper? I know that already. And how to serve things nobody likes when you have guests so you have leftovers for the next day . . . I know all that. That's why from now on I'm taking over the household.

MOTHER Am I to be your maid?

GERDA And I yours. We must help one another. Here's Axel.

* * *

SON-IN-LAW *(Enters with his cane)* Well, how's the sofa?

MOTHER It'll do . . .

SON-IN-LAW You mean you don't like it? Something lacking?

MOTHER I'm beginning to understand.

SON-IN-LAW Really! — — — Then in the meantime, since there's never anything to eat in this house, Gerda and I have decided to cook our own meals.

MOTHER And me?

SON-IN-LAW You're as fat as a tub. You don't need much; you ought to reduce a little, for your health, as we've had to do . . . And in the meantime, will you leave us a moment Gerda; in the meantime, you can light a nice fire for us!

    GERDA exits.

MOTHER *(Trembling with rage)* There's wood there . . .

SON-IN-LAW Oh no, just a few sticks, but you're going out after wood, a whole stove full!

MOTHER *(Hesitating)* Should we burn up our money?

SON-IN-LAW No, but wood you can burn, to keep warm. Come on now!

> *The MOTHER hesitates*

One, Two — Three!

> *The SON-IN-LAW hits the sofa with his cane.*

MOTHER I don't think there's any wood left . . .

SON-IN-LAW Either you're lying or you've been pilfering the wood money . . . because the accounts show that we bought wood the day before yesterday.

MOTHER Now I see what you are . . .

SON-IN-LAW *(Sitting in the rocking chair)* You would have seen that a long time ago if your age and experience hadn't duped my tender years . . . Come on now – get the wood . . .

> *The SON-IN-LAW raises his cane. The MOTHER leaves and returns with wood.*

SON-IN-LAW Now light it properly, and none of your games. — One, two, three!

MOTHER God, you're like him now, sitting in that chair.

SON-IN-LAW Light it!

MOTHER *(Calm rage)* I will, I will.

SON-IN-LAW Now you guard the flame while we go in and eat . . .

MOTHER What about me?

SON-IN-LAW Gerda will bring you a nice bowl of porridge.

MOTHER With blue skim milk . . .

SON-IN-LAW Since you consumed the cream, it's only right! And just!

MOTHER I'm leaving . . .

SON-IN-LAW You can't, I'll lock the door.

MOTHER I'll jump out the window.

SON-IN-LAW A good idea! You should have done that a long time ago and spared the lives of four people. Now light it — Blow on it! — There. Now you sit there until we come back.

>   *The SON-IN-LAW goes.*

* * *

>   *Pause. The MOTHER stops the rocking chair and listens at the door; then she takes a piece of wood out of the stove and hides it under the sofa. The SON enters a bit drunk.*

MOTHER *(Gathering her wits)* You?

SON Yes.

>   *The SON sits in the rocking chair.*

MOTHER How are you doing?

SON Bad. It's won't be long for me.

MOTHER It's only your imagination. — Don't rock like that! — Look at me. All my life I've lived and worked and slaved for my children and this household. Haven't I done that?

SON Ah! — The pelican that never gave her life-blood. Zoologists have proven that all that is a lie.

MOTHER Have you had any cause to complain?

SON Listen now mother, if I were sober I'd never answer that honestly, I wouldn't have the strength, but now I'm going to tell you: I read father's letter, which you stole . . .

MOTHER What letter? I don't know what you're talking about.

SON Always lying. I remember the day you first taught me to lie. I could hardly talk. Remember?

MOTHER No, I do not remember. Stop rocking!

SON And the first time you lied in front of me? — I was hiding under the piano when one of your cronies came to visit; you sat and lied nonstop for three hours, and I had to listen.

MOTHER It's a lie.

SON Do you know why I'm so worthless? A nursemaid and a glass bottle instead of mother's milk. And when I got a little older, the maid took me along to visit her sister, who was a prostitute. And there I got to see all the great secrets of life that only dog owners invite children to see every spring and fall on the street. When I told you about it, I was only four then, you said it was a lie and you beat me as a liar, even though I was telling the truth. Your maid, encouraged by this sign of assent, initiated me at five into the rest of the secrets. I was only five . . . *(He sniffles)* I began to get cold and hungry, like father and the rest of us. Now, for the first time, I know that you stole the household money and the wood money . . . Look at me, pelican, look at Gerda with her empty breasts – You know how you murdered my father when you drove him to despair, but that's not punishable by law. How you murdered my sister, you know that too. But now she also knows!

MOTHER Stop rocking! — What does she know?

SON You know, but I can't say it. *(He sniffles)* All this, it's terrible, but I had to say it. When I'm sober, I'm going to shoot myself, so I keep drinking. I don't dare sober up . . .

MOTHER More lies . . .

SON Father said one time in anger that you were the one great fraud of nature . . . that you didn't learn to talk as a child, only to lie . . . that you always avoided your duties in favor of parties. And I remember the time Gerda was sick, almost dead, you went to the opera — I remember your words: "Life is heavy enough without having to make it heavier." — — — And that summer, three months you were in Paris with father and partied the household into ruin while Gerda and I stayed here, locked in this apartment with the maid who soiled your bed with a fireman —

MOTHER Why haven't you spoken about this before?

SON You forget. I did and was beaten for gossiping, or lying, as you alternately called any true word you heard.

MOTHER *(Pacing the room like a newly caged wild animal)* Such words to your mother, I've never heard the likes of it.

SON It is a little uncommon, and completely against nature, I know, but for once it should be said. You were walking in your sleep and couldn't wake up, and that's why you couldn't change. Father said that if they put you on the rack you wouldn't be able to confess or even admit that you had lied . . .

MOTHER Father! Do you think he was faultless?

SON He had his faults, big ones; though not in his relationship with his wife and children. — But there were other secrets in your marriage which I imagined, suspected, but never chose to admit . . . Father took those secrets with him to the grave, partly.

MOTHER Have you said about enough now?

SON I'm going out to drink . . . I'll never take my exams. I don't believe in the legal system; the laws seem to be written by thieves and murderers to free the criminal; one truthful witness is not valid evidence but two false witnesses is full proof. At 11:30 I have an indisputable case, but after noon I've lost it. One slip of the pen, a misprint, a jot in the margin can land me in prison. If I'm charitable to some crook he has me punished for defamation of character. My contempt for life, for humanity, for society, and for myself is so immense that I haven't the strength to go on.

The SON goes to the door.

MOTHER Don't go.

SON Afraid of the dark?

MOTHER I'm nervous.

SON That figures.

MOTHER And that chair drives me crazy! Like two knives hacking away at my heart . . .

SON You mean you have one.

MOTHER Don't go! I can't stay here. Axel is a crook.

SON I thought so too until now. Now I think he's a victim of your criminal ways . . . The young man led astray.

MOTHER You must keep bad company.

SON Bad company? Yes, I've never had any other kind.

MOTHER Don't go!

SON What can I do here? Only beat you to death with my words . . .

MOTHER Don't go.

SON Are you starting to wake up?

MOTHER Yes, I am starting to wake up, like from a long, long sleep. It's terrifying. Why couldn't they wake me sooner?

SON What no one could do was probably impossible. And since it was impossible, you weren't responsible for it.

MOTHER Say those words again, please.

SON You couldn't have done any differently.

MOTHER *(Kissing his hand)* More.

SON No more — . Yes, one thing more. Don't stay here and make the pain worse.

MOTHER You're right. I will go.

SON Poor mamma.

MOTHER Compassion — for me?

SON Yes, for you. How often have I said: so much pain, so much evil, it's a shame.

MOTHER Thank you. — Go now, Fredrik.

SON It can't be helped, can it?

MOTHER No, it can't be helped.

SON No, it can't — be helped.

The SON goes.

* * *

Pause. The MOTHER stands alone for a long moment with her arms folded across her chest. She walks to the window, opens it, and looks down into the depths, then backs up into the room and runs toward the window as if to jump out; but she changes her mind when she hears three knocks on the rear door.

MOTHER What is it? What is it? *(She closes the window)* Come in.

The door opens.

Is there someone there?

The SON is heard roaring deep in the apartment.

It's him. In the tobacco barn. Isn't he dead? What should I do? Where shall I go?

The MOTHER hides behind the sofa. The wind begins to blow again like before. Papers fly around the room.

Close the window, Frederik!

A flower vase blows down.

Close the window! I'm freezing to death and the fire's gone out in the stove.

She lights all the electric lamps; closes the door, which blows open again. The rocking chair moves in the wind. She paces around and around the room until she throws herself on the sofa and hides her head in the pillows.

* * *

"Il me disait" plays in another room. The MOTHER lies on the sofa as before with her head hidden. GERDA enters with porridge. She turns off all the lights but one.

MOTHER *(Awaking and sitting up)* Don't!

GERDA We must cut costs.

MOTHER Are you finished already?

GERDA Axel gets bored without you. Here's your dinner.

MOTHER I'm not hungry.

GERDA Yes you are, but you don't eat porridge.

MOTHER I do sometimes.

GERDA No, never. But it's not because of that. It's for your nasty smile every time you tormented us with cornmeal. You enjoyed our suffering . . . and you fed the same stuff to the dogs.

MOTHER Not skim milk, it makes me shiver.

GERDA Since you skimmed the cream for your coffee — . *(Setting the porridge on a side table)* Eat it up now. I'm watching.

MOTHER I can't.

GERDA *(Taking the piece of wood from under the sofa)* If you don't eat, I'll show Axel the wood you stole.

MOTHER Axel? You just said he missed me . . . he won't hurt me. Remember at the wedding when he danced with me . . . Il me disait! There it is.

The MOTHER hums along as the second reprise plays.

GERDA It would be wiser for you not to drag up your scandals . . .

MOTHER And the verses and the poems and the most beautiful flowers.

GERDA Enough!

MOTHER Shall I recite it for you? I know it by heart . . . "In Ginnistan — — — " Ginnistan is a Persian word for the pleasure garden of Paradise where benign Peri live on perfume . . . Peri are genies or fairies who the longer they live the younger they grow . . .

GERDA Dear God, do you think you're a Peri?

MOTHER It said so. And Uncle Victor proposed to me. What would you say if I married again?

GERDA Poor mamma. Still sleepwalking like we all were, but will you never wake? Don't you see how people leer at you? Don't you understand when Axel insults you?

MOTHER Does he? It seems to me he's always more polite to me than to you . . .

GERDA Even when he raises his cane to you?

MOTHER To me? That was to you, dear child.

GERDA Poor mother, have you lost your senses?

MOTHER He missed my company this afternoon, we always have so much to talk about, he's the only one who understands me, and you, you're only a child . . .

GERDA *(Shaking her)* Wake up, for God's sake!

MOTHER You haven't grown up yet, but I'm your mother and have nourished you with my life-blood . . .

GERDA No, you gave me a bottle and a pacifier, and later I had to sneak into the pantry and steal, but there was only hard bread that I ate with mustard, and when it burned my throat I washed it down with vinegar.

MOTHER So, stealing even as a child. Very pretty, and you're not ashamed to talk about it? Imagine. And I sacrificed myself for such children.

GERDA *(Crying)* I could have forgiven anything. But when you took my life away from me — yes, my life, which began with him . . .

MOTHER Is it my fault he preferred me. Maybe he found me — how should I say, more pleasant. Yes, he had better taste than your father who couldn't appreciate my worth until he had rivals — — *(Three knocks are heard on the door)* Who's knocking?

GERDA Don't speak ill of father. I don't think my life will be long enough to make up for what I did to him . . . Remember, as a child, you taught me to sting him with words I didn't understand? He understood well enough not to punish me for those poison darts, he knew who bent the bow. Remember when you taught me to lie to him, to say I needed new books for school, and we'd split the money. — How will I forget the past? If I had the strength to leave, but I'm not Fredrik, a powerless sacrifice without a will, your sacrifice . . . you . . . too hardened to suffer for your own crimes.

MOTHER Do you know anything about my childhood? Can you imagine the kind of home I had, what evil I had to learn? It seems to go on, passed down, from above, from where? Our first parents the children's books said. There seems to be something to it . . . Don't blame me and I won't blame my parents who won't blame theirs and on and on. Besides, it's the same in all families, though it doesn't show from the outside . . .

GERDA If so, I don't want to live, and if I'm forced, I shall go blind and deaf through this vale of tears, hoping for something better . . .

MOTHER Always exaggerating, my dear, when you have a child of your own you'll have other things to think about . . .

GERDA I won't have any children . . .

MOTHER How do you know that?

GERDA The doctor told me.

MOTHER He's mistaken . . .

GERDA More lies . . . I'm sterile, underdeveloped, like Fredrik, and that's why I don't want to live . . .

MOTHER Such talk . . .

GERDA If I could only do the evil I want to do, you would cease to exist. Why is it so hard to do evil? When I lift my hand against you, I only strike myself — — —

> *The music stops suddenly. The SON is heard in another room roaring.*

MOTHER Drinking again.

GERDA Poor Fredrik... what can he do?

* * *

The SON enters half drunk and stammering.

SON I think... there's smoke... in the kitchen.

MOTHER What's he saying?

SON I think... I think... I... it's burning!

MOTHER Burning? — What are you saying?

SON Yes, I do believe... it's burning.

The MOTHER runs to the rear door and opens it but is met by a wall of flames.

MOTHER Fire! We've got to get out. — I don't want to burn. — I won't!

GERDA *(Embracing her brother)* Fredrik, run, the fire...

SON I can't...

GERDA Run. — You must.

SON Where?... No, I can't...

MOTHER The window... I'd rather...

The MOTHER opens the balcony door and jumps.

GERDA Oh God, help us. —

SON It was the only way.

GERDA You've done this.

SON What else could I do? — There was no choice. — Was there? Another way?

GERDA No. Everything must burn. It's the only way out. Hold me, Fredrik, hold me hard, little brother. I'm so happy, happier than I've ever been. It's getting light. Poor mamma, she was so bad, so bad . . .

SON Little sister, poor mamma, feel how warm it is, so warm, I'm not cold now. Listen, the beams are cracking, all the old is burning away, everything painful and wicked and ugly . . .

GERDA Hold me tight, little brother, we won't burn, we'll be smothered by the smoke, so soft; the smell, so good. That's the palms and pappa's laurel wreath, and now the linen closet, smells of lavender, and now roses. Little brother, don't be afraid. It's soon over, dear, dear, don't fall, poor mamma. So bad. Hold me, harder; hug me, like pappa used to say. It's like Christmas when we got to eat in the kitchen, lick the gravy on our fingers, the only day we ate our fill, as pappa used to say. Feel the aroma. It's the pantry, the tea box, and coffee, and spices, cinnamon, clove . . .

SON *(Ecstatic)* Is it summer? The clover is in bloom; summer holidays are beginning, remember when we went down to the steam boats and stroked the fresh white paint, waiting for us, and pappa was so happy, he felt alive he'd say and no more exams. Life should always be like this, he'd say, and the seagulls circling overhead and the pelican sitting on the tie-post; he always had patches on his knees and worn out collars, and we were dressed like royalty . . . Gerda, hurry up, the ferry bell's ringing. Mamma's waiting on the foredeck. No it's not her — mamma. You'll be left behind. Poor mamma, is she still on the dock? Where is she? I can't see her. Wait. It's no fun without mamma. Oh, there she comes — Now, now the holidays begin.

> *The rear door opens. The red glare is intense. The SON and GERDA fall to the ground.*

Curtain.

END!

The Black Glove
A Lyrical Fantasy
(for the stage)
in five scenes

Opus 5 of the Chamber Plays (1909)

The Black Glove

Characters

THE YOUNG WIFE.
THE CONSERVATOR. Called "Old Man" in the text.
ELLEN.
KRISTIN.
THE CARETAKER.
YULE-TOMTE.[1] Called "Tomte" in the text.
CHRISTMAS ANGEL. Called Angel in the text.
AN OLD WOMAN.

1. Vestibule.

>*Upstage, a door with a letter box and name plate: to the right an icebox; to the left a bench. Above the door is a colored window with the image of a heart.*
>
>*A black glove lies on the vestibule floor.*
>
> *
>
>*An OLD MAN enters from the left out of breath. He sits on the bench. He glimpses the glove and picks it up with his cane.*

OLD MAN What's this? — A glove? Black, woman's size six. It belongs to the young wife in there. I can tell by the marks from her rings; left-hand two plain ones and on the ring finger a rose-cut diamond. A pretty hand, but with a tight grip, silken paws with sharp nails. I'll put it here on the ice box, and it'll find its way back to where it belongs. *(As the CARETAKER enters from the left)* Good morning, old friend, and merry Christmas.

CARETAKER Merry Christmas to you, Conservator. That is you, isn't it?

OLD MAN Yes, it is I. Birds I preserve, and fish and insects, but I can't preserve myself — even if I put arsenic soap under the skin, it'd still wrinkle, and the hair falls out like on an old sealskin trunk, and the teeth go …

CARETAKER It's like the electricity here, constantly needing updating and repairs …

OLD MAN Bad luck we have to sit in the dark on Christmas. Can't you get the lights working?

CARETAKER There seems to be a short, but it can be fixed — let's have a look … *(Flips a switch and the heart window lights up)* See, now there's light in the hallway — — —

OLD MAN You spread light throughout the house — — —

CARETAKER But down in the cellar I live in darkness. There's only the kerosene lamp —

OLD MAN It's good to live for others! — My goodness how beautiful that heart is!

CARETAKER It is beautiful, but the color's harsh! Sharp you could say!

OLD MAN Like the young wife! If only she were as good as she is beautiful!

CARETAKER What's this glove here?

OLD MAN It was lying here in the vestibule. Do you think maybe you could take care of it?

CARETAKER I'll take it along and hang it up on the board downstairs until the rightful owner shows up — now up I go.

OLD MAN And I'll sit here a little longer and rest my 80-year-old bones … Merry Christmas.

CARETAKER *(Turning off the heart and going out to the right)* Merry Christmas!

*

> ELLEN enters from the right, opens the icebox and takes out a rack of milk bottles.

OLD MAN Good morning, Ellen, and merry Christmas.

ELLEN Merry Christmas, Conservator.

OLD MAN And how is the little one, and the young wife?

ELLEN Oh, those two, they chirp together like canaries — you can hear them all the way out here. But between you and me — — — the wife isn't very nice to others. None of us, including the caretaker, got anything extra for Christmas. She says we're all beasts — — —

OLD MAN You shouldn't be talking about such things to me. I'm not part of the household — they'll say I'm a gossip — — —

ELLEN Speaking of canaries, have you been able to stuff that canary of hers yet?

OLD MAN Yes, yes I have. — But — *(Hesitating)* she won't pay me — well, now I'm spreading gossip.

ELLEN No, she won't pay for work — and when the master wanted to give us girls something extra for helping them move in from the country — she was furious. — When he gave it to us anyway, she left the water running and the electricity on the whole night. — And when she didn't get her way, she made herself sick — like she was going to die, and the master had to send out for the doctor. And when he came it was nothing but a sham. She talked about poisoning herself and threatened to turn on the gas and blow the whole building up.

OLD MAN God preserve us. Is that what your life is like in there?

ELLEN But between times, she's like an angel of peace. — You should just see her playing with her child, or when she sits and sews her Christmas presents, like she's doing now. — It's like she's beset by bad powers when it happens, and she shouldn't be blamed for that, the poor thing.

OLD MAN That's nice of you to say, Ellen. I should think she must be ill. I've seen it before … They have it too good and that's the illness. The husband's rich and doesn't have anything to do.

ELLEN But he's busy all day long, trying to spend his money. This year he's refurnished the living room three times, once in black pear wood with silver, and it all went up into the attic. As you say, they have it too good.

*

KRISTIN *(Entering from the right, talking softly)* What are you doing here, Ellen? She's beside herself. A ring's disappeared …

ELLEN Which ring?

KRISTEN Her favorite. The one with the blue stone that cost 2000 crowns — and when she missed it, she immediately thought —

ELLEN What?

KRISTEN That you'd run off and taken the ring with you.

ELLEN No — I've never heard the likes. Me? What do you think, Kristin?

KRISTIN I know you're not guilty — when you know someone, you can tell right away: that one is guilty, that one isn't.

OLD MAN Is it so easy?

KRISTIN One wouldn't swear to it, but one can still be certain.

ELLEN And so I've been fired?

KRISTIN It's like an obsession with her …

ELLEN But she can see I haven't run off.

KRISTIN That doesn't help.

ELLEN And if the ring shows up, she'll be mad at me for being innocent and because she was wrong. You know, I think I'll just leave.

KRISTIN No, don't go. That will convince her and she'll send the police after you.

ELLEN Well, it's going to be a fine Christmas in this house.

OLD MAN *(Getting up)* You girls will have a nice Christmas, after the testing — after the rain, the sun always returns — and so it will be here too. Ellen, you're an honest girl, but you must learn to be patient.

ELLEN Haven't I already learned that?

OLD MAN Yes, but there's still more to learn! — So let me say it again, wholeheartedly and as a pledge: merry Christmas, my girls.

>*The OLD MAN goes out to the right.*

*

ELLEN If only having a clear conscience were enough.

KRISTIN It goes a long way. Come in now, but be calm and patient when the storm breaks.

ELLEN How am I supposed to do that?

KRISTIN Look at the master of the house. He's a suspect too.

ELLEN Him too?

KRISTIN Him too. But he doesn't storm around or get angry, only sad. — Now come back in.

ELLEN Him too. Then it's no shame on me. So I can bear it.

KRISTIN Come in now.

>*They go out to the right.*

*

TOMTE *(Entering with a broom)* Now I'll sweep up for Ellen and Kristin, 'cause they're nice; but their neighbor Ebba gets the sweepings, 'cause she's nasty; and I'll dry the bench and the icebox, and polish the brass — but not Ebba's! So there now. — Now let's have a look what's going on inside.

>*The TOMTE turns on a flashlight: the back wall is lit from behind and we can see into the entry hall: a white icebox with a white mirror above, a little white stool with a pair of child's galoshes underneath; the YOUNG WIFE stands in front of the mirror fixing her hair.*

TOMTE Yes beautiful little mother, you're welcome to admire those gifts you've received, but you mustn't adore them. You're welcome to love your little child, but you mustn't idolize her. Now a Christmas card from me. *(Searching through a bundle of cards)* Alpine rose? No. Violet? No. Snowberry? No. Mistletoe? No. Thistle? Yes, that's for you. A beautiful flower but thorny. *(Putting a card through the mail slot)* Now let's hear what they're saying in the kitchen. *(Turning off the flashlight and listening toward the right)* Ellen is accused of stealing a ring. — She didn't do it! Ellen, take a ring! Now Ebba could have. I know everyone here in the house. All the fine folks and all the serving girls. Ellen's crying. I'm going to look for that ring from cellar to attic, in the elevator, in the washing room, in the vacuum cleaner. I know every nook and cranny — — — let me just check and see that they're keeping the icebox tidy. *(Looks in the icebox, rummaging around)* Yes, that will do.

*

ANGEL *(Dressed all in white with snowstars in her hair)*
What are you doing, you little nuisance?
Standing there listening? Now isn't that nice.

TOMTE What the tomte does is always right.
He's master of order here in the house,
He chastises and comforts, abuses and loves, and he cleans.

ANGEL It's a vast house to look after.

TOMTE A Tower of Babel with all manner of folk
And all manner of language. Six stories high and a cellar;
Three flats per story; a dozen cradles and seven pianos,
And many a fate has been met here.
It twists and it buckles in minds and hearts and souls
Like beams set in stone;
It holds together, but that's about it;
And neighbors who don't know their neighbors
Need concessions and consideration,
Need to tolerate others' little caprices.
Someone plays the piano after ten,
Someone gets up too early or goes to bed too late!
It can't be helped; adjustments must be made.
Hear those little noises in the stairwell chatter!
Now the elevator creaks, and the water pipes rattle,
And the radiators whistle like a teakettle.
Now there's the shower and now the vacuum cleaner;
There's a door slamming and a little one crying!

Here a newlywed, there a divorcee, over there a widow.
All on top of each other like their pianos
Playing a waltz, a fugue, a sonata.
In the cellar poverty, as in the attic;
In the flats luxury and vanity.
Solid investments and cavernous lives —
They muddle through, they rush forward, they scrape along.
Someone dies one fine day, another marries, another separates,
Someone quarrels, complains, patches it up,
But when he sees that one more fight does no good
He packs up and leaves in the end.

ANGEL Who lives in there?

TOMTE The little wife whom everyone talks about.

ANGEL I know her then, I'll bet! —
Listen what a storm's coming from the kitchen! —
No, dear child, is this the peace of Christmas?

TOMTE On the day before Christmas eve
Things always heat up in the kitchen.
But there's something else going on here too:
Poor Ellen's unjustly accused …

ANGEL I know, and that's the last drop;
Now the cup of mercy runneth over
And the wine of wrath shall be pressed from sour grapes,
Though to punish is not my domain.
I comfort, I aid, I set things right again;
But you can pull their hair, you have strong hands …
Now listen! That little woman created in beauty
To give joy to people and glory to the Giver,
Must be taught a lesson, hard but brief —
She's built her happiness on her little child,
And on that happiness she's built conceit …
Well then, take away the child
So she'll know what it feels like to lose something —
But never fear! She'll get her back again tomorrow evening
As a Christmas gift; but as a gift, mark it well.
What will they think? Let them think what they want.
That the child's disappeared? Gone missing?
But you mustn't lie to them
A single false word sprouts like weeds! …

TOMTE It's too cruel, she'll never manage.

ANGEL She will. I'll stay near her.
Her heart is not bad, only sickly a bit;
And sorrow will cure her in time. —
When the blazing sun of happiness glares down,
The grass and flowers wither;
A little cloud brings shade and comfort
And it also brings rain, and with rain comes the greening — — —
Now the clouds are gathering. — But don't handle her too roughly.

TOMTE *(Sadly)* Do you have to ask this of me? —
She's so beautiful!

ANGEL Yes, and will be good.
And then know real happiness — the kind that lasts.

TOMTE But just a minute, up there in the attic I have
A poor man who's waiting for a gift —

ANGEL Who is your ward, just say the word.

TOMTE He's a philosopher who longs for the end.

ANGEL Over life and death we have no power
But if he's deserving, he'll receive a gift.

TOMTE He ruminates over the mystery of life —

ANGEL Is that something to ruminate over? —

TOMTE He's an old ninny, but kind …

ANGEL What's he doing up there in the attic, then?

TOMTE He stuffs birds, dries fishes, sticks worms on a board,
And has a cabinet full of yellow paper.
And he searches in that cabinet, night and day;
Searches for the mystery of life.

ANGEL I know the type. Well, he shall have his Christmas gift. —
But now, merry Christmas and off to work you go.

Curtain falls for a moment.

2. Entry hall.

Entry hall. A white icebox to the right with a white mirror above; on a shelf under the mirror is a silver brush, and a glass vase with tulips. Under the mirror hangs a basket for gloves. On the icebox sits the TOMTE's Christmas card with the thistle. To the left is a white stool and a place to hang coats. Under the stool is a pair of child's galoshes. A child's white fur coat and winter hat are hanging up. No other clothes are seen.

In the back, a door opens into a sitting room. Through a yellow curtain a sewing table can be seen with a beautiful lamp. Beyond an arrangement of beautiful flowers stands the young wife. She is dressed in white, with a square-cut collar; her black hair sits on the top of her head, Japanese style, showing off her neck. She is sewing a piece of yellow cloth, which could be part of a child's garment.

TOMTE *(In the entry hall, taking the Christmas card from the icebox)*
So there's my Christmas card with the thistle —
A little weed in the wheat you'll have —
It pricks like you, but has a beautiful flower! —
Like you, pretty little mother! —
Look at her hand, as if she were picking flowers;
And her head bowed as if in meditation or prayer. —
Now she smiles: she hears her baby coming —
Tiny steps on shining parquet tiles
Polished yesterday with beeswax and pine oil. —
It smells like a pine forest in May when braxen jump on the lakes —
And the green shutters of the summer cottage are opened. —
A beautiful home where beautiful people live beautifully,
Protected from the dirt of life. —
Look at the flowers by the mirror —
Tulip turbans of red and yellow,
Hiding round cheeks and blossoming lips
That meet in chaste kisses. —
Like those the water lily gives its mate on a lake's shallow mirror. —
Ah yes, the mirror! And the marks of little fingers
Searching for the image behind the glass,
Thinking there must be another little girl.
And there sits Rosa on her mistress's chair,
Guarding the girl's coat and her dear little boots;
Everything to sweeten life and home
Is here behind closed doors —
But goes unnoticed until it's lost. —

Now turn off the light so darkness hides the sorrow.
What I must do can't bear the light. —
(Turning a switch on the wall — darkness)
But when this light is lit again, we'll have Christmas in the house.

> *The TOMTE hides behind the curtain on the right. The YOUNG WIFE rings a little bell. ELLEN enters with a lighted candle. The YOUNG WIFE scolds her. ELLEN cries in the entry hall and goes out.*

> *The YOUNG WIFE comes into the entry hall with a candle, which she sets on the icebox. She finds the Christmas card with the thistle, which she reads and then tears up. Afterwards she looks in the mirror and fixes her hair. A neighbor plays the "L'istesso tempo di arioso" section of the third movement of Beethoven's Sonata 31, op. 110 on a piano. The YOUNG WIFE listens. Then she takes the silver brush and begins to brush the child's clothes; she brushes and picks off lint. Noticing a loose button, she takes the doll from the chair and puts it on the icebox; then she sits on the chair, takes a needle and thread from her bosom and sews the button back on. The YOUNG WIFE stands and picks up a black glove from the glove basket: she searches for the match but can't find it; she looks in the child's galoshes under the stool. She gives up and puts the glove in her bosom.*

> *The music changes to Beethoven's Funeral March. The YOUNG WIFE listens, gripped with fear. There is a noise from the icebox as if a block of ice has fallen.*

> *A child screams. The YOUNG WIFE is terrified and wants to leave, but stands stone still.*

> *There is a pounding in the wall; the elevator grumbles, the water pipes rattle; the murmur of voices can be heard through the wall.*

> *KRISTIN enters, ashen-faced with her arms lifted and her hands clasped. She talks quietly to the YOUNG WIFE and hurries out.*

> *The YOUNG WIFE wants to run after her but can't — she falls to her knees next to the chair and hides her face in her child's coat, which she caresses and hugs to her.*

> *Curtain falls for a moment.*

3. At the Caretaker's.

> *The CARETAKER's room. In the back, a colored window lit from outside though occasionally obscured as the elevator goes up and down.*
>
> *A Christmas table[2] with a white tablecloth and a small Christmas tree with wax tapers; at one end of the table sits a half-keg surrounded by scattered fir branches; rolls, a butter dish, a pig's head, a shoulder of mutton, half a cured salmon, a roast goose etc. A traditional three-branched candle sits on the other end of the table: juniper branches on the floor; on the wall a color print of the birth of Jesus; under it, keys hang on a black board. A kerosene lamp is lit.*
>
> *The CARETAKER sits at the table, resting.*

OLD MAN *(Entering with a yule sheaf[3] under his arm)* Hello again, my friend. Sitting here alone?

CARETAKER The tree won't grow old unless it's alone in the forest
Unconstrained by the young;
And time has thinned things out passably well around me.
(Pause. Inviting the OLD MAN to sit)
Once my house was so full, we were packed in —
I'm not complaining; it was warm and fine with mother and children.
But this is fine too, perhaps even better;
Everything is best in its own way and its own time …
I sit here now in the shade of my Christmas tree
And remember what's past with a grateful heart.
I had it all, indeed! How many others who haven't
Trouble themselves with missing what they never had;
And now it's too late to get it. —

OLD MAN Yes, I have also had … but I'd rather not remember —

CARETAKER Sit with me a bit. I should have said
As a man from the country, from Bergslagen,[4]
I'm free. — I was raised under the earth in the mines;
So I get along just fine down here,
Hidden in the cellars of the Tower of Babel. —
I see daylight through the colored window,
Which is my sun, though darkened now and then
By the shadow of the elevator passing by like a storm cloud.

OLD MAN You sit here like the Old Man of the Mountain,[5]
Ruling over all the elements —
Master of fire and warmth; parsing out water, cold and warm;
Spreading light through the dark regions;
And by expanding and compressing the air
You suck up the dust of the world that has gathered
On the wandering feet of the children of men;
And by regulating the laws of gravity you make the elevator
Rise or sink with a wish.

CARETAKER That's enough of that, my friend.

OLD MAN Oh come now, you're much more besides. —
I see you have the keys to all the doors in the building,
And all have the key to your heart.
You know all the destinies woven here;
You hear it all, you see through walls,
You reach down to the bottom of things.
And to you they bring their confidences,
their worries and their sorrows — — —

CARETAKER You give me too much credit, good doctor,
But I can hear it without getting spoiled or scared.
You've made me more content with this little place;
You've cheered me up when I was depressed
And changed this cramped little room into a palace!

OLD MAN They're talking out in the vestibule, raised voices …
Someone's yelling, someone's crying; soon they'll be in here
And you must sit as judge; straighten things out, give advice,
Quiet them down when they make a scene.

CARETAKER *(Listening)* It sounds like the lovely Ellen —
From the third floor — maid to the young wife …

OLD MAN I will take my sheaf and go up to my birds.
They're having a singing contest with the weathervanes.
— And so I bid you a merry Christmas

CARETAKER And the same to you, doctor.

OLD MAN One word more. How did it go with that glove you found?

CARETAKER Ah yes. I must have lost it on the stairs — ,

It's not a big problem. Who will miss a glove?

OLD MAN Don't be too sure: like seeks after like.

> *The OLD MAN exits.*

*

> *ELLEN enters, dressed to go out.*

ELLEN May I sit here with you for a minute, Caretaker?

CARETAKER Sit my child.

ELLEN I can't take it anymore; when the electricity went out, I got blamed, and now I'm being accused of taking that ring; they're reported it to the police. —

CARETAKER And this is Christmas? You're the worst ones I have in this house — but first let's have some light. *(Gathering up his tools)* My hammer, my pliers. *(Taking some keys from the board)* So I can go through locked doors —

ELLEN I think the heating has gone out too.

CARETAKER That too! What's going on up there? You're the only ones this happens to.

ELLEN It's betrolled — . I got frightened, heard a child scream, and there was playing in the walls. — Kristin's probably leaving too. She can't take it either.

CARETAKER Where's the master then? Is there no man at home?

ELLEN I think he's gone away hunting — we haven't seen him for two days — he couldn't take it either. But it's like the Conservator says: they have it too good. Nothing to do, no appetite, no wish to sleep. Their only worry is what to do with their money.

CARETAKER Though they don't pay for work. That they won't do.

ELLEN So you haven't gotten a Christmas gift either?

CARETAKER Oh no. She got mad at me because I asked her not to stand there in the elevator — yes I suppose I said it a bit sharply of course, because I was in a hurry.

ELLEN Quiet, I hear Kristin on the stairs. — She's more tolerant than I am, but even she gets tired — .

CARETAKER Just think: for some riches aren't a blessing. — There's comfort in that for us poor folks, though small comfort. Where did they get their money?

ELLEN They must have inherited it. — Quiet, she's here. Something else must have happened up there on the ghost-floor. —

CARETAKER Ghost-building rather. For so many strange things happen here. — It's like all these machines brought something in with them. — Ebba says she's seen a tomte sitting on the roof of the elevator holding onto the lines —

* * *
*

The TOMTE is seen mixing up the keys on the board.

ELLEN A person could really begin to believe in spirits, for sometimes you don't find something where you left it, sometimes a door locks itself, sometimes warm water comes out of the cold spout — — —

CARETAKER *(Listening)* Is there someone here? I thought I heard the keys rattling. *(The TOMTE hides)* Some devil must have mixed up these keys. — Here's number 25 on 13 and 17 on 81. And the grocer's letter is in the district judge's slot. And there's always voices in the stairwells. They quarrel and cry, but when I go out to look, there's nothing —

ELLEN But this time it's Kristin — you can tell by the way she walks.

CARETAKER *(Looking out the door to the left)* Not a living soul here —

ELLEN Now I'm getting frightened — . Sometimes it's children's voices — sometimes it's doves on the roof — sometimes I think it's the Conservator sitting up there making fun of us — . Who is he really?

CARETAKER He's a strange fellow — but there's no harm in him — .

ELLEN Listen, you haven't found a glove on the stairs have you?

CARETAKER Yes, the Conservator found it, and I was supposed to look after it, but I seem to have lost it.

The telephone rings.

CARETAKER *(Into the telephone)* — Yes, she's here. — No, that's not possible. She didn't take any ring. We know Ellen. She'd never take anything. — It's unjust. But I'll tell her, yes. — Yes, yes.

The CARETAKER hangs up the phone.

ELLEN I know. — It was the police.

CARETAKER Yes, my child. They want to talk to you.

ELLEN I'll throw myself in the lake.

CARETAKER But go to the station first.

ELLEN Never. You never get out again.

CARETAKER Look at me — Ellen — and don't believe that harm will come to you. Go now in peace.

ELLEN *(Looking at him, she is convinced)* I'll go. — I looked into your eyes, I heard your voice. — Now I feel safe and can go. *(As the CARETAKER leads her out)* And this hand gives me strength. — It leads me, it supports me. — I'll go.

ELLEN goes. Pause.

*

OLD WOMAN *(Entering with a black glove and a little child's brown boot)* Look what I found in the elevator! Perhaps you can find their owner — — — Did you get your Christmas gift from me?

CARETAKER Yes, thank you. And the glove that went missing.

The CARETAKER sets the glove on the table with the boot.

OLD WOMAN A Christmas table with a tree — and so much food— smoked pig's head! Thanks be.

CARETAKER And the rich envy the poor.

OLD WOMAN Maybe you're not as poor as you seem. Nor I as rich. — — — Take care of that glove now — so it doesn't get lost again. — It's a black one — as black as a funeral — but it conceals a white hand and maybe something more.

>   *The OLD WOMAN goes.*

CARETAKER *(Dumbfounded)* "Little boot with worn down heel; Tramped upon with too much zeal … "

*

>   *The TOMTE snatches the glove and hides.*

*

CARETAKER It's a child's — boy or girl? No way to tell. They haven't decided between right and left yet — nor between right and wrong. — They are of the kingdom of heaven still — but later. Oh yes. — *(Reaching for the glove)* Now where's that glove? I put it here on the table. *(Searching)* Gone.

KRISTIN *(Coming into the room, distraught)* Just think, just think …

CARETAKER What is is? Who is it? — Kristin!

KRISTIN Just think. God help us. — The baby is gone.

CARETAKER Gone? What do you mean?

KRISTIN Disappeared. Someone's taken her …

CARETAKER Impossible. I would have seen. I would have heard. I'm here to guard the house and the people who live here.

KRISTIN You know nothing about it? Then I'm going to the police. — Be kind to the mother if she comes down. She's been sitting up there without light or heat. — — — It's just too terrible. Even for the likes of her.

>   *KRISTEN goes out.*

*

CARETAKER What is all this? Not the work of man, for sure. There's hope in that. *(Setting the boot on the table)* Who's coming? It must be her, the poor little mother.

The CARETAKER conceals himself to the right.

YOUNG WIFE *(Entering from the left, dressed as in the first scene)*
Where have I come to? And where am I?
What have I come from? And who am I?
A poor man lives here. — But look at all those keys.
Must be a hotel. — No, a prison, a dungeon. —
There's the moon, but it looks like a heart,
And black clouds stride past. —
There's a forest, a pine forest,
A Yule forest full of gifts and light. —
In prison? This is strange. Is no one here?

CARETAKER *(Can be seen in the right corner but only by the audience. Speaks in an aside.)*
She's beside herself, she's lost her memory —
A blessing for someone who suffers .

YOUNG WIFE But quiet! I remember; but the memories are back there
And I've come here to look for something.
What am I looking for?
A glove I lost. It was black — Now it's black again.
But in the darkness I see something blue,
Like the sky in spring between white clouds;
A mountain lake between steep shores.
The sapphire I lost was that blue — That someone stole —
I've lost much these past days —
Froze so in darkness — Here it's warm but close;
The weight of high towers above
And the heaviness of human destinies all around,
I feel them pressing me down to earth —
And squeezing my heart in its feeble cage. —
I want to speak but search for words
I want to cry as if I had some sorrow.
(Taking the boot) What's this? — A little boot.
A little stocking and a foot. In you go. —
What's this? — A candle that's shot out branches,
It's grown from the root of the trunk and soon it will blossom:
Three bluish white flowers, with red inside — — —
Who would have thought a candle could grow, shooting out branches!

What part of the world is this I've come to?
An anchor bouy floats in a pine forest,
A wild boar rears up from the waves,
And fish walk on dry land! —
(Seeing the print of the birth of Jesus)
What's this? — A crib in a stable.
(Beginning to awaken)
And the brown cows of the shepherds kept watch with their large eyes
Over the little child — who — slept in the manger — .

The YOUNG WIFE wakes and screams.

O dear Jesus, savior of the world, save me. I'm lost. I — am — lost! — A child is born this night, a child is dead. There's the caretaker. He's angry with me for not getting a Christmas gift. Don't be angry with me. Don't take revenge. I'll give you all my rings …

CARETAKER *(Coming forward)* I'm not angry, I don't want revenge. Your child will return again. A child can't just disappear in a city like this. — Come with me and I'll get you some light and heat in the meantime —

YOUNG WIFE Say that again, that a child can't disappear. — I don't believe a word of it, of course — but say it again anyway. Say it over and over again.

CARETAKER Come with me, while I fix the machines, then you can go up and warm yourself at an old friend's, three stories up. He's good at talking — I'm not— and he will comfort you —

YOUNG WIFE Do you mean the Assessor? He's angry with me too?

CARETAKER No one here is angry with you. — — — Now come along.

YOUNG WIFE How nice he is; and no wish for revenge.

CARETAKER Oh my, oh my, how wicked you are.

YOUNG WIFE But my baby. — My child.

CARETAKER Come.

Curtain.

4. The Attic.

> *The attic: Two windows in the back covered with light green curtains; between the windows is a manuscript cabinet with a beautiful lamp on it; to the left an oak table covered in papers; to the right an arm chair.*

*

TOMTE *(Entering)* It's Christmas Eve morning,
But in the old philosopher's room, not a trace of Christmas cheer.
 (Drawing aside the curtains) He's put his Christmas tree on the balcony
For the sparrows and doves;
And from the thousand yellow beaks of grain
One kernel each to feed the birds of heaven,
Sleeping still on the metal roof
With their heads tucked under their wings. —
Soon the morning breeze will shake the weather vanes
On the chimneys over the stoves
Where the fires burn cheerily heating up the coffee pots. —
Then I'll skip along the gambrel roofs
And delight in the smells —
As the morning sun casts its rays through the telephone wires
And the wires sing with the weather vanes,
And the doves grumble in their cornices
And children leave their beds — — —

What's he got here?
On yellow sheets of paper in the thousands
He's gathered all he knows.
Straw collected under hothouse litter, thoroughly threshed,
Where one must search for the kernels of grain —
And the kernels he's collected here in this barn
Of burnished oak. Here lies the harvest —
(He opens the cabinet)
And here's the registry, the key to his wisdom:
To the secret of creation, which he believes he has found —
Everything in order, you old fool. —
Now I'll stir up the rubbish you've gathered in the hills;
And create chaos once again
So you'll have to start from the beginning.
(The TOMTE mixes up the manuscripts)
These must be the wise man's spectacles;
With the years he's grown short-sighted. —

A Christmas gift from me you'll get
That'll make you far-sighted, and foresighted!
(*The TOMTE exchanges the glasses with another pair that he takes out of his pocket.*)
You'll get new eyes
To see what can't be seen
By mere mortals in everyday life;
Where before you saw laws
Now you shall meet the lawgiver,
And later the Judge;
Where before you saw nature
And the botherment of blind chance,
Now you'll find beings of the same sort as you.

I hear the old man waking —
Perhaps he was keeping watch;
For the nights are like days
For those who probe in the darkness.
Now he's coming, I'll stay,
And make his acquaintance,
And he can make mine.

> *The TOMTE conceals himself behind the drapery on the right. The OLD MAN enters from the left, dressed in dark clothes, a white scarf, and a black skullcap. His hair and beard are long.*

OLD MAN Welcome life. Good morning toil.
For sixty years I've ordered the cosmos —
Now has risen the morning sun of the day
On which I shall unlock the riddle. —
Everything lies there like layers in the earth,
Deposited slowly through fire and water—
Of stones, and grasses and animals,
Ur-elements, powers, measures and numbers.
I've dragged together the building blocks
Of the Tower of Babel's heavenly stairs.
With it I shall climb from this vale of tears
And take this mosque with me, with its blue copula[6]
Resting on the four points of the compass —

For sixty years I've gathered and counted;
And once, halfway along, I found the riddle. —
It was at night, and I wrote it on a scrap of paper —
But it got buried, and has since disappeared. —

It's here someplace, but as I've searched
The pile has grown into a haystack,
My own child has grown into a giant ...
As soon as I advance I'm beaten back,
I dig as one digs for treasure,
But the spade falls from my hands,
My head tires, my body withers,
And I lie here as if dead
When I had hoped the entirety to survey. — — —

Now I feel the moment has come,
For in a dream last night
I saw the paper I've sought:
Blue-white, Regal-size of English manufacture — .
(Takes off his cuffs)
Now or never! It's you or me.
You paper mountain, give up your secret,
I am your master!
All you spirits, here I command.
(Puts on his glasses and rummages around in the papers)
What's this? What's this?
I can't find my old order:
Letters and numbers have changed places,
A, B, C, D, H, R — it's like the very —
And numbers 1, 7, 4, 10, 26, — Someone has been here!
Alpha, Beta, Pi. And the cipher I had discovered
I have forgotten. — It's disappeared from my memory. —

(Continuing to rummage around) Here's a lead — but in the middle is a splotch of ink. *(Taking up a knife)* I'll scratch it off. Now there's a hole in the paper. — Great! I'll go on searching. *(Searching page by page)* I'll go through every sheet one at a time and I will find it —

The neighbors are starting to play. — Play on. — It doesn't disturb me, I have the whole day — and the night too. I don't eat — and require no sleep.

> *As the OLD MAN digs in the papers, a piano is heard playing for a few minutes: Beethoven's Sonata 29, Op. 106, Adagio Sostenuto.*

Tired so quickly today? — I'll just rest a minute.

> *Miserable, the OLD MAN falls into the easy chair; the music continues.*

My eyes are so strange; what's near wanders into the distance, and what's far away seems nearer. My head is empty.

> *The OLD MAN closes his eyes. The music continues. The OLD MAN wakes and attacks the pile of papers again. But tires almost immediately and returns to the chair. He attacks again but is repelled. He sleeps in the chair as if dead.*
>
> *The TOMTE pushes in a chair from the right and sits obstinately across from the OLD MAN. The music stops. The OLD MAN wakes.*

OLD MAN Who's there? Are you real …

TOMTE To be is to be perceived;
You see me, so I am.

OLD MAN *(Getting up)* But I want to touch you, to hold you;
Otherwise you don't exist for me.

TOMTE You can't touch the rainbow, but it exists.
Or a mirage at sea or in the desert exists. —
I am a mirage; don't come too near
Or you'll stop seeing me, even though I still am.

OLD MAN Actually, your logic makes sense …

TOMTE Then you're bound to believe your own eyes — .
(The OLD MAN grumbles.)
You grumble, because I'm not part of your system;
Your system is your lord, and you are its drudge.

OLD MAN I reign supreme in my system — .

TOMTE Then tell me succinctly the guiding thought
Behind all the facts you've gathered here,
Otherwise all you have is a pile of leaves,
Of raindrops, of grains of sand,
Which are each like the others and not like them at all.

OLD MAN My thought, my idea that holds together
The millions of phenomena we meet —

TOMTE Let's hear it. I'm so anxious to learn.

OLD MAN You little thief, you've stolen my thought;
It was all so clear just now — — —

TOMTE And now? It's gotten cloudy
Like crystal-clear ice during a thaw;
It's turned to slush and then water, which flies off in a mist!
The mist has gone. I'll condense it again
And tell you the system you've forgotten.
(Pause) In the unity of the Eternal you can see the world's riddle — — —

OLD MAN Precisely! You are a cleaver little guy
Who found what I've sought for thirty years.
The unity of matter. That's the word.

TOMTE That's the system. Now back to reality.
Ponder now nature's duality. And let's see
If this theory has anything to it.
(Pause) The wet element, water,
Is a unity composed of two:
Of hydrogen and oxygen, it can't be disputed;
Magnetic power is divided between North and South;
Electricity is positive and negative;
The seed of the plant is both male and female;
And highest in the chain at the very top
You find duality, for it was not good for man to be alone —
And so came man and woman forth —
And the duality of nature was confirmed.

OLD MAN You little devil. Now you've plucked it all asunder —

TOMTE Your toy, you big silly, your chain has snapped
Into a scrapheap of scattered links;
The cable you twisted together has come apart
And now it's so much junk for the trashman —

OLD MAN Ha! Sixty years to blow a bubble
That in a draft of wind has burst.
There's no point now in living any longer.

TOMTE If the bubble has burst, you can blow a new one.
They're made of water and soap suds
Whipped up to look immense
But really are so little, next to nothing —

OLD MAN And sixty years —
(Getting up, angrily, he throws the papers into the wings to the left)
Out of here! You damn delusion!
The rotten fruit of twenty thousand days of work.
Out! Out! You dried leaves, which have eroded my tree;
Friar's lantern, wandering flame that led me astray,
Taunted me into the swamp where I sank in the mud to my neck,
Lured me into the desert,
Where thorny bushes tore my hands — .
(Emptying the cabinet of paper, but leaving a box)
Get out you false pilots that drove me aground,
Guides that pointed the way to hell!
Bankrupt, fallen, I relinquish my station
And sit empty-handed on a burned plot of land —
(Sinking down into the chair)
A snail whose shell has been crushed,
A spider whose web's ripped apart,
A bird that has flown too far out to sea,
Too far to turn round and come back to shore —
He wings over a churning abyss —
Until he tires and falls — to his death.

    Pause.

TOMTE Tell me — Would you like to start over? Become young again?

OLD MAN Become young? No thank you.
Regain the strength to suffer —
The strength to weave false dreams? No!

TOMTE Is it gold you want?

OLD MAN I want nothing — except to be allowed to go hence.

TOMTE Yes well, first you must reconcile with life.

OLD MAN Reconcile? — Be bound again to the stake? —
Absolutely not! Or there'll be no departing —
"A last handshake and one for the road?"
"Stay a bit longer" — and then you're left behind — .
No, get up on the goat, whip the nag,
Tear yourself loose, and no turning back.

TOMTE You tore yourself lose once from life,

From hearth and home, from wife and child,
To run after honor's empty eggshell —

OLD MAN Half true — I left in time to keep from seeing the others go;
They'd packed and were ready.
When life deceived, when the ship was about to sink,
I made myself a lifeboat and blew it up with air,
That much is true. It held me up a while, a pretty long time,
But then it burst and I sank. Am I to blame for that?

TOMTE *(Taking the box from the cabinet)*
Here's some flotsam the sea has returned —

OLD MAN *(Powerless)* Leave my box alone. Don't wake the dead.

TOMTE You don't believe in resurrection, you Sadducee —
Why do you fear the dead?

OLD MAN Leave that box alone. You'll call up spirits —

TOMTE Indeed. So you'll see that life is spirit
But imprisoned in a body, in matter.
Now pay attention, I'm calling them up.
I'm conjuring, I'm summoning.

The TOMTE opens the box.

OLD MAN Ah! What is that fragrance? Clover blossoms
In rosy May when the apple trees burst forth
And the lilac spires sway in the westerly wind,
And the newly dug gardens,
Which had just now lain white with snow
Stretch their black attire over buried seeds
Waiting in the soil to be reborn —
(Sindling's "Frühlingsrauschen" can be heard)
I see a little cottage, white with green shutters.
A window is open, the curtains flutter —
Wine red taffeta. — And furthest in the back
An Empire mirror in a gilded carved frame —
And in the oval glass of that mirror, as if a mirage,
I see the most beautiful thing life can offer:
A young mother dressing her child,
Combing her soft hair, washing the sleep
From her blue eyes which open to smile

At the sun and at her mother, with the pleasure of living — .
The frolicking little foot stamps on the carpet,
Impatient as a colt to be free to run out —
Music! The notes of earlier days half-forgotten rise up again —
The little stream glides past the alders;
A boat, midsummer crowns, baskets of wild strawberries,
And fresh pike squirming on the hook —

> *The TOMTE takes up a little bridal crown and white veil.*

What do I see? What have we here?
A little crown of myrtle with a gossamer veil;
A little princess and a fairy dance in the morning mist at sunrise — .
But I can see no more, my eyes shroud over. —
Dear God, all of this once was,
But is no more, and never will return.

> *The OLD MAN weeps.*

TOMTE All of this once was yours and you threw it away,
Fresh flowers for dried leaves;
Warm life for cold thoughts.
You poor man — . And what have I here?
(Displaying a black glove)

OLD MAN A little glove! Let me see. I can't remember —
How did that get in there? — Wait, yes — Now I have it —
Yesterday morning I found it on the stairs —

TOMTE And now you can have it as a Christmas gift from me —
It holds secrets, and those slender fingers
Have meddled in destinies, caused harm;
But this little hand stretches out to you for good — .
If you will give it to her as I expect,
You will have spread happiness, solved a riddle
Worth more than that Sphinx's riddle that's been clawing at you —

> *The TOMTE locks the box in the cabinet.*

OLD MAN Can I still make another happy?
Can I receive a grateful glance?
Can I give comfort, move a heart?
Then a cure for despair might have a chance.

TOMTE Your ancient forest dark and dank you've burned;
It was the bravest and the smartest thing you've done.
Sow now on the burnt-out plot of land,
Since things grow well in ashes:
A few harvests still you can bring in.
And though you won't yourself enjoy the fruit,
You can give it all away.
For it's more blessed to give than to receive,
And sacrifice makes us happy — .
(Pause) I must return now to my desolate eyrie,
But wish you first a Yule most merry.

    The TOMTE disappears.

*

OLD MAN *(Alone, considering the glove)*
A little hand that reaches out in the darkness —
A gauntlet thrown in peace not battle.
A child's hand, soft and tender —
What kind of secrets do you hide?
Could it be you're a premonition
Of what's to come as Christmas gifts? —
(A knock on the door)
Come in, unseen friend, a Christmas gift awaits
Whoever comes first. — Come in.

*

ELLEN *(Entering)* Forgive me, Doctor, for coming in like this,
But you're known as a friend to all. —
I am lost, abandoned, in despair.

OLD MAN *(Getting up)* God comfort you, my child, sit down.
What's happened? Is it about the ring?

ELLEN I've been there and I'm still suspected;
They're looking for me now.
I wanted to drown myself in the sea
But I couldn't. Let me stay here;
Say something. Say "innocent."

OLD MAN Be calm, and let me think a minute —
What was it again? —

A Christmas present from a stranger.

ELLEN An old glove?

OLD MAN I don't understand either;
But it was lost and found,
Lost again, and found again —

ELLEN I think it's my mistresses'. Let's see the size.
(As ELLEN turns the glove, the ring falls out.)
Dear God! The ring! I'm saved!
You didn't know about this?

OLD MAN I didn't know. Dry your tears.

ELLEN How kind you are. That you are kind to animals
And flowers I knew already — — —

OLD MAN Quiet now. I had no part in this.

ELLEN Is it not good to rescue another?

OLD MAN I was only an instrument, not the giver.

ELLEN Be happy now, I wish I were you,
Able to make a poor girl happy —

OLD MAN Go and set right what you can,
And be happy with the rest of the household . . .

ELLEN
What can I do? — The little child is gone.
How shall we find happiness in this house of sorrow?

OLD MAN The child? Yes, I heard the story —
But believe me, Ellen: someone's playing hide the ring —
More I don't know. But looking at it another way
I believe, I hope, I trust that before the day is done
The testing time for each of us will be fought and won.

The OLD MAN sinks down in the chair and falls asleep.

Curtain

5. The Child's Room.

> *The Child's Room. In the back a beautiful alcove curtain with a little table before it: on the table two candles in silver candle sticks; between them a portrait of the child with flowers; a mirror behind the candles reflects their flames.*
>
> *To the left, a white crib with a blue "sky" above; to the right, a child's table with a small chair. On the chair sits a doll, Rosa; on the table, Christmas presents and a little tree. A white rocking horse sits next to the bed.*

YOUNG WIFE *(Entering, dressed in a black pelisse and wearing a black veil, from which she tears off pieces and hangs them on objects in the room: the Christmas tree, the doll, the rocking horse, etc.)*

Bereavement greets us,
But something more fills the emptiness;
We have been given cold, and the cold chills us;
We have been given darkness, and the darkness conceals
Like a blanket one creeps under during sleepless nights
To escape the nightmare's images.
Rosa, do you miss your little mistress?
Your cheeks are so pale, and your hands so cold:
Shall the Christmas tree play its funeral dirge?
(She winds up a music box and sets it under the tree.)
And Blanka the Horse wears mourning ribbons on her arm.
I remember last year when we went out
To visit mother and father in the country.
You stood all alone in this cold room.
But Mary didn't forget you:
"Poor Blanka must be freezing
And maybe she's afraid of the dark all alone in that room."
When she came home you had caught a cold,
Had a sore throat, and she cared for you;
Wrapped her best stockings around your neck,
Kissed your white nose, and combed your mane,
And wrapped a golden ribbon round your forehead.
Yes, you had it fine, you did, but now —
Now we have it bad, so bad, all of us.

Little crib, you're empty, like a lifeboat rocking empty
On the waves of the sea after the ship has sunk — .
Who will I make the bed for? My little life is dead?

I remember the last evening after supper
When you got crumbs in your bed and I had to remake it;
You said it was sand left by the sandman.
I used to mix fairytales and lullabies
With your evening prayers
To lull you along on your voyage
To the green forests and blue lakes of dreamland — .
Your eyelids would close like daisies
Over your rosy cheeks, under the fairy grass of your hair — — —
No longer there! A little, little hollow in the soft pillow
Is all; an impression of your little body —
In under the bed's blue sky.
Now it's black and covered with clouds — — — .
Where is my child? Where are you? Answer.
Have you gone to the stars
To play with other children not yet born,
Perhaps dead and born again?
Have you gone in search of fairy tales?
And met Thumbelina, and the Blue Bird,
And Red Ridinghood and little Soliman,
Having tired of us and our squabbles?

I so want to come along! I've never felt at home here —
It promised everything, but didn't keep its promises.
All as if but never was;
An art work, perhaps, but one badly done.
Too much body, too little soul.
And how miserable that one could not be,
Could not become, what one most wished to be.

(Pause) But it's dark, closed off from the light —
(The YOUNG WIFE flips a switch but nothing happens.)
And it's cold, they forbid me heat.
(The YOUNG WIFE stretches out her hand as if looking for a faucet)
And no water. My little flowers are thirsty.
(The YOUNG WIFE rings a little bell.)
But no one comes. Everyone has gone.
Was I so wicked then? No one knows
What everyone knows — or everyone thinks they know!
Everyone bowed to me and no one dared say
How I ought to behave.
Yes, the mirror dared, but it was a bad friend —
Its smooth glass spoke only nicities —

(Pause) What's this here? — The glove I dropped!
And here, in the finger, is my ring!
Then she wasn't guilty, poor Ellen.
Now she will be revenged, and I will bear her punishment.
And the last shall be worse than the first! —
In jail? — I won't — I'll hide the ring —

(Pause) Oh! — What was that? Someone slapped my cheek!
Is someone here? — I heard whispering.
A child breathing in its sleep —
And now! The weathervane on the neighbor's roof — .
Hush, listen. He's singing up on the chimney crown — .
What is he saying? "My Mary, Mary, Mary!"
And then: "Ellen, Ellen!" — Poor Ellen! — — —
An alarm bell rings! The ambulance!
What can have happened? What have I done?
No. Right must be right, and when I have erred
I must go myself and take my punishment.

ELLEN enters. The YOUNG WIFE falls on her knees before her.

ELLEN Sweet Jesus, get up! I am so sorry, poor thing, unhappy mistress dear, get up, I can't bear to see you like this; it was nothing, a mistake. These things happen; everything is so rackety. It's hard to live; next to impossible, someone has said. So, so.

YOUNG WIFE Ellen, forgive me.

ELLEN I already have, I have, dear one; now stand up and I will tell you something ...

YOUNG WIFE *(Rising)* Is it about — — — ?

ELLEN No. But it's about someone else. The old man who lives in the attic — he's passed on — reconciled and satisfied with what he had wished for — . But when we searched in his papers, we found his true name — And ...

YOUNG WIFE Then I know. — He was my lost father.

ELLEN Yes.

YOUNG WIFE And he died without seeing his child again. — I must go to him. — This peculiar house, where the destinies of men are stacked floor upon floor, one upon another, and next to each other, one after another — Where is my husband? Has no one heard from him?

ELLEN He will be home for supper — but not before.

YOUNG WIFE For Christmas dinner? In the dark and the cold. In this house of sorrow, this room of the dead. — My poor husband. — I must go up to my father — . Ellen, how did he die?

ELLEN He burned his papers and said it was all a pile of scrap — and it was he who found the ring. — When he had made me happy, he said: Now I can die satisfied, having had the honor of making another happy.

YOUNG WIFE He was right. — I didn't love him; but I will close his eyes and perform the final services, as one should. Come with me Ellen.

> *ELLEN and the YOUNG WIFE go. Pause. KRISTIN and the CARETAKER, with his tools, walk slowly across the stage.*

CARETAKER Things are sorting out, sorting out.

KRISTIN *(Pointing to the crib)* Shhh!

> *KRISTIN and the CARETAKER slip out. The TOMTE appears from the right, the ANGEL from the curtains on the left.*

ANGEL We're nearly finished with our task —
I saw a kneeling, heard a tone of voice,
That little word "forgive" can settle all.
Now it's been said, now it's been done. —
Put sorrow aside! Let the feast of happiness come!

TOMTE *(Sneaking around to gather up the mourning crape)*
I blow the dust away, I sweep and clean,
I polish the brass that's been clouded by foul breath;
I water the flowers when the maid forgets so they won't be thirsty.
(Watering the flowers by the mirror)
The curtains I straighten in pretty pleats,
And pull the carpets straight;
I can bring disorder too, but not here, and not today.
Beautiful young wife, dear little mother,
Now that you've suffered, don't forgot your lessons!
Tears of regret and pain make your eyes
Shine so beautifully clear and mild;

But when you cry with anger, you grow ugly.
Now, angel? Now can we say, "Merry Christmas"?

ANGEL She comes from a service of love,
From closing the eyes of her father —
Who got his child back again in death —

> *The TOMTE goes and looks in the crib, rocks it gently, lifts a finger to his lips as if to say: "she sleeps."*

Now she will get her child back in life —
Go tend to the switches and toggles and spigots.

TOMTE I go and make everything ready for the final tableau!

> *Each leaves in a different direction.*

*

YOUNG WIFE *(Entering as before in her pelisse)*
O blessed warmth! Have you returned?
A southern wind — has the winter sun risen from the equator?
Is it summer?

> *Lights come up to full on the stage. The YOUNG WIFE drops her pelisse on the floor.*

Oh God — One word — And there was light!
Have you opened your heavens again,
So I may see a little visage smiling between white clouds,
Small hands stretching out, a little mouth — — —
But hush!

> *The YOUNG WIFE listens as if she hears a sound from the crib. She looks around.*

And here! What's happened? Has grief passed?

> *The YOUNG WIFE goes to the crib and sees the child, not seen by the audience.*

Yes. The Lord taketh away and the Lord giveth again.
I am not worthy of such mercy yet —
(On her knees by the crib)

But when a mother has her child back in her arms.
There are no words for happiness, and happiness weeps.

> *The TOMTE can be seen taking off his hat and throwing kisses to the mother and child from the right curtains.*

> *Curtain.*

> *The End!*

Notes

Introduction

1. (p. 6) The demise of the Intimate Theater was brought on by a fight between Strindberg and Falck because the later had put on a production of a play by Maurice Maeterlinck. Strindberg who was funding the theater with his own money and the money of his supporters felt that although he admired Maurice Maeterlinck, the Intimate Theater needed to stay devoted to Strindberg's work. Strindberg was famously easy to offend and what to Falck seemed like a minor disagreement resulted in the end of their partnership and friendship.

Translator's Note

These translations are based on Vol. 58 of *August Strindbergs Samlade Verk*, edited by Gunnar Ollén (Stockholm: Norstedts, 1991). I have tried to follow Strindberg's idiosyncratic punctuation for the most part with one notable exception. I have tempered Strindberg's over fondness for exclamation points because the presence of exclamation points tends to encourage modern actors to yell a lot. At this point in his career, Strindberg seems to have been experimenting with punctuation as a guide to phrasing.

Storm

1. (p. 7) **"Pluie d'Or":** Also called "Pluie de diamants," this popular waltz was composed by Emile Waldteufel in 1879. "Alcazar" or "The Spanish Waltz" was composed by Otto Roeder. "Alcazar" is also mentioned in Part One of Strindberg's *The Dance of Death* (1901). *The Saturday Review* for 18 November 1893 noted that "Spanish waltzes seem to be in vogue at present, and their liveliness is certainly an agreeable relief from the languorous casino style of the past." I doubt, however, that the same would have been said more than a dozen years later, when Roeder's waltz would have sounded old-fashioned and perhaps even cloyingly sentimental.

2. (p. 22) **Chopin's *Fantasie Impromptu Opus 66:*** This composition for piano is one of Frédéric Chopin's best-known pieces and is also heard at the opening of *The Pelican*. In a letter written on 25 April 1907 to his brother Axel, Strindberg provides some suggestions for transcribing

Chopin's piece. Chopin's *Nocturne* appears in Strindberg's final play *The Great Highway* (1909).

BURNED HOUSE

1. (p. 63) **C'est vrai:** Strindberg has the Stranger use several English words and phrases in the play, including here ("It's true"). Since the Stranger was a world-traveler I have chosen to put this phrase, in French.

2. (p. 64) **Our country's great warrior:** The reference is to Charles XII of Sweden (1682–1718), whom Strindberg saw as epitomizing the corrupting abuse of absolute power. In 1901, Strindberg wrote a remarkable play entitled *Karl XII* about the warrior king who expanded the Swedish empire at the expense of the Swedish people.

3. (p. 70) **Humbug:** Here and elsewhere Strindberg uses the Dickensian "humbug" in English. Because James Carpenter, who played the Stranger in the Cutting Ball Theater's production, has for years played Scrooge in the American Conservatory Theater's annual production of *A Christmas Carol* and is closely associated in the minds of San Francisco audiences with the role of Scrooge, we changed this for the San Francisco production to "Rubbish."

4. (p. 74) **I just couldn't distinguish between the names:** In fairness to the painter, it should be noted that "red" (*röd*) and "green" (*grön*) in Swedish share the same vowel, making them more similar in Swedish than in English.

5. (p. 85) **Smoke and mirrors:** I have followed Gunnar Ollén's useful suggestion in his notes to vol. 58 of *August Strindbergs Samlade Verk* (1991) that "*de blå dunster*" refers to the cloud of blue smoke that magicians use in their magic shows.

THE GHOST SONATA

1. (p. 92) **The Porter:** Strindberg lists this character in the *dramatis personae* though he doesn't appear in the text of the play.

2. (p. 93) **Advertising column:** In his opening stage direction, Strindberg mentions an *Affisch-Kolonn* but not the *telefonkiosk* that appears later in the scene. Advertising columns (called *Colonne Morris* in French and *Litfaßsäule* in German) became popular in major cities across Europe in the second half of the 19th century after being introduced in Germany in 1855. Public telephone kiosks were introduced in Stockholm during the

1890s, though they looked nothing like "advertising columns."

3. (p. 93) **Gossip-mirror:** A *reflexionsspegel* or *skvallerspegel* is an angled mirror attached to an outside window frame that lets people in the house watch people passing by on the sidewalk. Often two mirrors are attached at a 45° angle so someone in the house can see what's happening on the street in both directions.

4. (p. 97) **The Valkyrie:** In Richard Wagner's *Die Walküre* (1856), the second part of his cycle *The Ring of the Nibelung*, the heroine Brünnhilde is stripped of her immortality for defying the god Wotan and trying to protect the condemned Siegmund. *Die Walküre* was first performed in Stockholm in November 1895.

5. (p. 101) **Spruce branches:** Traditionally, *granris* were strewn on the threshold of a house where a body was being prepared for burial.

6. (p. 102) **English Amazon garb:** What seems like a bit of Strindbergean misogyny was in fact a common term for a woman's riding habit at the time. The dictionary of the Swedish Academy (*Svenska Akademiens ordbok*) cites usage of the term *amasondräkt* as early as Erik Wilhelm Weste's *Svenskt och fransyskt lexicon* (1807).

7. (p. 107) **The ass in the well and the corn in the field absolve us:** Here Director Hummel alludes to two New Testament passages: Luke 14:5 and Mark 2:23-28.

8. (p. 121) **Kakadora! Dora!:** Gunnar Ollén, in his notes to vol. 58 of *August Strindbergs Samlade Verk* (1991), points out that this onomatopoeic sqwauk plays on the Swedish word for "cockatoo" (*kakadora*).

9. (p. 122) **Song with Prelude:** Here and at the end of the play Strindberg paraphrases stanzas from the 13th-century Icelandic Christian poem "Sólarljóð" (Sun Song).

10. (p. 131) **Böcklin's "The Island of the Dead":** Swiss Symbolist painter Arnold Böcklin painted at least five different versions of *Die Toteninsel* ("The Island of the Dead"), which was one of Strindberg's favorite paintings at the time. Copies of Böcklin's "The Island of the Living" and "The Island of the Dead" hung on either side of the proscenium arch in Strindberg's Intimate Theater. In March 1907, after completing *Ghost Sonata* and abandoning and burning another proposed Chamber Play called *The Bleeding Hand*, Strindberg began work on a play entitled *Toten-Insel* (subtitled "Hades"), inspired by Böchlin's painting. By late

April he had lost interest in the play, as he wrote to his German translator Emil Schering, "just as I have lost interest in life, and suspect the end is near." *Toten-Insel* remained unfinished. Instead Strindberg turned to *The Pelican*, which he completed in June 1907.

THE PELICAN

1. (p. 151) **Godard's *Berceuse de Jocelyn*:** The *berceuse* from Benjamin Godard's 1888 four-act opera *Jocelyn* (Op. 100) is a kind of lullaby with alternating harmonies that gives it a kind of lulling or rocking effect. Berceuse in French can also mean "rocking chair."

2. (p. 155) **Camorra:** The Neapolitan secret crime syndicate, organized along lines similar to those of the Sicilian mafia, came to prominence during the 19th century and was associated in the public mind with anarchist attacks in France during the final decades of the century.

THE BLACK GLOVE

1. (p. 176) **Yule-Tomte:** A *tomte* (derived from the Swedish word *tomt*, "a plot of land on which a house or farmhouse is built") is a kind of house-spirit who watches over and protects a local household or farm, particularly at night, bringing luck and happiness to the inhabitants and guarding them from misfortune. The *tomte* is said to be the size of a child but with an ancient, intelligent face. He dresses in gray jacket, short pants and small clogs covered in pitch (i.e., in clothes typical of an 18th-century farmer). In 1881, Victor Rydberg published a popular poem entitled "Tomte," illustrated by Jenny Nyström, that transformed the tomte into a philosophical guardian of the spirit of Christmas (*Jul*).

2. (p. 187) **A Christmas table:** Here Strindberg presents a typically Swedish Christmas table with seasonable foods and the three-branched candle (*grenljus*) traditionally associated with the season.

3. (p. 187) **Yule sheaf:** When the harvest was over, a sheaf of the finest grain (*julkärve*) was set aside to be tied with a ribbon to a tree or high pole at Christmas time for the birds. Some thought that honoring the birds at Christmas would persuade them not to disturb the grain in the fields before it was harvested in the summer.

4. (p. 187) **Bergslagen:** Inhabitants of the iron mining region known as Bergslagen, north of Lake Mälaren in northern Svealand, were known for their distinctive dialect and cultural independence.

5. (p. 188) **Old Man of the Mountain:** The *bergkung* or king of the mountain is best represented in Ibsen's *Peer Gynt*. Legend has it that on Christmas Eve the troll king opens his hall, illuminated by the light of a thousand torches and supported by pillars of gold, to passersby who are trapped in the mountain when the magical entrance into the hall closes suddenly.

6. (p. 197) **"This mosque … with its blue copula":** In 1908, a year before writing *The Black Glove*, Strindberg had moved into a new ultra-modern apartment in downtown Stockholm. The building was known as the "Blue Tower" because of its great blue copula.

7. (p. 202) **Sindling's "Frühlingsrauschen":** This refers to Christian Sindling's solo piano piece "Frühlingsrauschen" Op. 32, No. 3 (The Rustle of Spring).

Cast and Production Team

These translations of the Chamber Plays of August Strindberg were premiered by The Cutting Ball Theater in the fall of 2012 in San Francisco, the first time all five Chamber Plays had ever been presented together.

The translations of *Storm*, *Burned House*, and *The Black Glove* were commissioned and developed by The Cutting Ball Theater.

Storm Cast

The Gentleman	James Carpenter
The Brother	Robert Parsons
Confectioner Starck	David Sinaiko
Mrs. Starck	Anne Hallinan
Agnes	Caitlyn Louchard
Louise	Ponder Goddard
Gerda	Danielle O'Hare
Fischer	Carl Holvick-Thomas
The Iceman	Michael Moerman
The Postman	Paul Gerrior
The Lamplighter	Alex Shafer
The Delivery Man	Nick Trengove
Milkmaid	Anne Hallinan

Burned House Cast

The Dyer	Robert Parsons
The Stranger	James Carpenter
The Mason	Paul Gerrior
The Old Woman	Gwyneth Richards
The Gardener	David Sinaiko
Alfred	Nick Trengove
The Stonecutter	David Sinaiko
Matilda	Caitlyn Louchard
The Hearse-Driver	Alex Shafer
A Detective	Michael Moerman
The Painter	Paul Gerrior
Mrs. Vesterlund	Anne Hallinan
The Wife	Danielle O'Hare
The Student	Carl Holvick-Thomas
The Witness	Ponder Goddard

The Ghost Sonata cast

Director Hummel	James Carpenter
The Student	Carl Holvick-Thomas
The Milkmaid	Ponder Goddard
The Concierge	Gwyneth Richards
The Dead Man	Paul Gerrior
The Lady in Black	Danielle O'Hare
The Colonel	Robert Parsons
His Daughter	Caitlyn Louchard
The Mummy	Gwyneth Richards
The Nobleman	Alex Shafer
Johansson	Michael Moerman
Bengtsson	David Sinaiko
The Fiancée	Anne Hallinan
The Cook	Anne Hallinan
The Beggars	Nick Trengove
	Alex Shafer
	David Sinaiko

The Pelican cast

The Mother	Danielle O'Hare

The Son	Nick Trengove
The Daughter	Caitlyn Louchard
The Son-in-Law	Carl Holvick-Thomas
Margaret	Gwyneth Richards
The Testing Powers	Ponder Goddard
	Anne Hallinan
	David Sinaiko

The Black Glove cast

The Young Wife	Danielle O'Hare
The Conservator	James Carpenter
Ellen	Caitlyn Louchard
Kristin	Gwyneth Richards
The Caretaker	Robert Parsons
Yule-Tomte	David Sinaiko
Christmas Angel	Ponder Goddard
An Old Woman	Gwyneth Richards

Production Team

Director	Rob Melrose
Scenic Design	Michael Locher
Costume Design	Anna Oliver
Lighting Design	York Kennedy
Sound Design	Cliff Caruthers
Props Master	Sarah Bingel
Dramaturgy	Bennett Fisher
Stage Management	Jocelyn A. Thompson
Production Management	Heather Gallagher
Assistant Director	Amy Clare Tasker

The Cutting Ball Theater

Artistic Director	Rob Melrose
Associate Artistic Director	Paige Rogers
Managing Director	Suzanne Appel
General Manager	Laura Mason

About the Translator

PAUL WALSH is Professor of Dramaturgy and Dramatic Criticism at the Yale School of Drama. Prior to coming to Yale, Walsh taught theater history, dramaturgy and dramatic literature at the University of Massachusetts Amherst and at Southern Methodist University (Dallas). He served as senior dramaturg at San Francisco's American Conservatory Theater (A.C.T.) from 1996-2005, and as Artistic Director of the New Harmony Project, a new play development residency program in southern Indiana, from 2006-2012.

Walsh's translations of Ibsen's *A Doll's House* (2004), *Master Builder* (2006), and *Hedda Gabler* (2007) have been produced at A.C.T., Yale Repertory Theater, Williamstown Festival, People's Light and Theater, Aurora Theater, and by the Chesapeake Shakespeare Company, among others. His translation of August Strindberg's *Creditors* has been produced by A.C.T., Actors Theatre of Louisville, and Kitchen Dog Theater after premiering at the Classic Stage Company in New York in 1992. These translations of August Strindberg's Chamber Plays were produced in repertory by San Francisco's Cutting Ball Theater in the fall of 2012 as part of the international Strindberg year celebrating the 100th anniversary of the author's death.

Walsh has worked as dramaturg with theater companies across the country, including the Minneapolis-based Theatre de la Jeune Lune, with whom he collaborated on such award-winning projects as *Children of Paradise: Shooting a Dream*, *Don Juan Giovanni*, *Germinal* and *The Hunchback of Notre Dame*. The version of Charles Dickens's *A Christmas Carol* that Walsh co-authored with A.C.T. artistic director Carey Perloff has played at A.C.T. since 2005.

After completing a master's degree in English literature at the University of Minnesota in 1978, Walsh received a guest fellowship from the Swedish Institute to study at the University of Uppsala in Sweden. He continued to live in Sweden for several years before enrolling in the doctoral program at the Graduate Centre for the Study of Drama at the University of Toronto, where he received a Ph.D. in drama in 1988 with a dissertation on the early works of August Strindberg.

More Plays From EXIT Press

Woyzeck, Pelleas and Melisande, Ubu Roi: translated by Rob Melrose "Rob Melrose is a kind of magician, and his theater, Cutting Ball, is one of the most exciting and integrity-filled enterprises going in the sometimes-shabby field of the American theater. These translations, lucid and sharp, are a beautiful testimony to the value of Rob's achievement." — Oskar Eustis

Ten Plays by Mark Jackson "From reimagined Shakespearean classics (*R&J, I Am Hamlet*) to Jackson's breakout hit *The Death of Meyerhold*, the bleakly comedic *American $uicide*, and the stirring Kurosawa-esque epic *The Forest War*, what these plays have in common is an audacious commitment to the illimitable possibilities of live theater" — Nicole Gluckstern, SF Bay Guardian

Songs of Hestia: Plays From the 2010 San Francisco Olympians Festival Playwrights Nirmala Nataraj, Bennett Fisher, Stuart Eugene Bousel, Claire Rice, and Evelyn Jean Pine adapt some of Western culture's oldest stories, illuminating our present-day concerns with imagination, creativity, curiosity and passion.

Snakes of Kampuchea by Mark Knego A trilogy of plays about Cambodia, the Khmer Rouge, resettling into San Francisco's Tenderloin neighborhood, and returning to your homeland. Includes *Snakes of Kampuchea*, *Tual Kan's Journey*, and *Return to Angkor*.

EXIT Press is the publishing division of EXIT Theatre, a San Francisco theater company that was founded in 1983. Coming soon are *Three Plays* by Mark Jackson, *Plays from the 2011 San Francisco Olympians Festival* and books of plays by Elisa de Carlo, Sarah McKereghan and Sean Owens.   www.exitpress.org

www.ingramcontent.com/pod-product-compliance
Lightning Source LLC
Chambersburg PA
CBHW032040150426
43194CB00006B/366